EDUCATIONAL

ADVANCED SUBSIDIARY

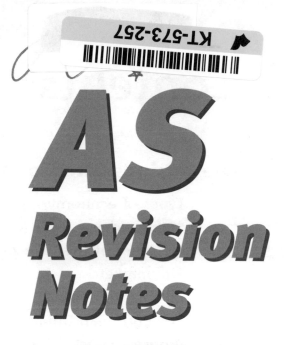

AS
Revision Notes

Business Studies

Author

David Floyd

Contents

The business environment

Classification of business

External and other influences

Structure and efficiency

Accounting and finance

People in organisations

Marketing

Operations management

The business environment

Types of economy

The market economy

- In a true market economy (**free enterprise**), resources are privately owned, production decisions being made by **entrepreneurs**, and not by the state on behalf of its people.
- The **profit motive** affects demand, supply, and price.
- The **Price Mechanism** allocates scarce resources, changing prices, giving signals, and acting as incentives to buyers and sellers.
- Although the market economy is efficient in producing and allocating resources, collusion between producers, incomplete price knowledge by consumers, restrictions on entry to new firms, and taxes/subsidies limit economic efficiency in practice.
- The price mechanism and profit motive can mean social judgements are ignored, and the state will have to intervene to provide non-profitable services (e.g. universal health care, defence).

The command, or planned, economy

- All costs are considered, the **central planning authority** taking into account social and other costs not easily measured in financial terms.
- **Public goods** are provided, being made on the basis of need rather than profit – but the lack of a profit incentive gives little encouragement to innovate and be efficient.
- Because prices are less influenced by demand/supply interaction, there are fewer price signals for producers.

The mixed economy

- Public and private sectors co-exist in a mixed economy.
- The distinction between these sectors is based on **ownership**, as well as on how resources are allocated.
- In practice, both sectors may produce the same item: e.g. health services in the UK are provided by both public (the NHS) and private (e.g. BUPA) sector organisations.
- All businesses in a mixed economy:
  - must meet the needs of **stakeholders**
  - require **finance**
  - need **people** (employees, customers, suppliers).

Examiner's Tip

Both 'pure' market and planned economies do not exist in practice, countries having a mixed economy to allocate their scarce resources.

Stakeholders

The nature of stakeholders

- Stakeholders are individuals or groups that **influence**, or are influenced by, an organisation's decisions.

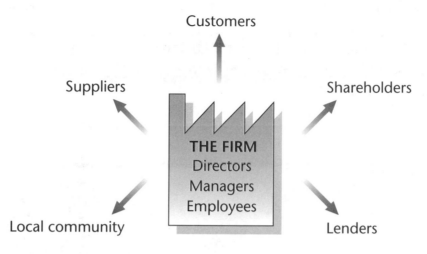

Figure 1.1 Stakeholders in a firm

Possible conflict

- The organisation's directors and managers face a possible conflict between their **duty to stakeholders** and their **duty to shareholders**.

- Directors, employed by shareholders, may feel obliged to undertake policies for the benefit of the shareholders. This **shareholder concept** may imply that policies which maximise share price and dividend are followed at the expense of other policies.

- Other stakeholders' objectives may conflict with this: there may also be conflict between the objectives of any two stakeholder groups.

- As an example, after establishing closer links with a supplier, a company may start using a new manufacturing process that affects its relationships with the local community.

- Stakeholders' objectives therefore affect the **behaviour** and **decisions** of an organisation.

Stakeholder and policy/action	Benefit
Close involvement with local community	Good publicity for the firm; support from local community when needed
Improving working conditions for employees	Improved morale and motivation; higher profits; reduced labour turnover
Better links with suppliers and lenders	Good long-term relationships; better communication; better quality

Examiner's Tip

In the longer run there may not be conflict: improved quality and efficiency brings higher profits.

Structure of the UK economy

The three sectors

- **Primary**: extractive industries such as fishing, forestry, farming, mining and quarrying.
- **Secondary**: firms involved with manufacturing and construction.
- **Tertiary**: service providers, both **commercial** services, e.g. banking and retailing, and **direct** services, e.g. health, education.

The UK economy

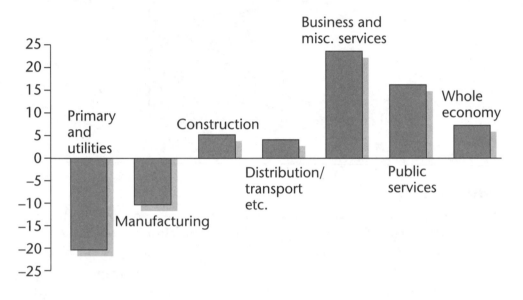

Figure 1.2 *Sectoral employment projections, percentage change, 1991–2000*
Source: Department for Education and Employment, 1996

- The move from primary and secondary production to tertiary production confirms the **de-industrialisation** of the UK economy.
- Reasons for this include the fall in the UK's competitiveness in secondary production, and the growth of newly industrialised competitors, such as the 'tiger economies' of the eastern Pacific rim (e.g. Taiwan, South Korea).
- This is typical of other developed Western economies, whereas a number of developing economies are still experiencing a major shift from primary to secondary production.

Examiner's Tip

These trends in the UK economy affect firms' organisational culture and strategy, and how they manage change.

The markets

What is a 'market'?

- It is a meeting of **buyers** and **sellers**, where goods/services are exchanged for other goods and services.
- This system of **exchange** is based on demand, supply and price.
- A **consumer market** buys and sells consumer goods: an **industrial market** buys and sells producer goods.

Demand

- The fundamental law of demand is: **price up = quantity demanded down; price down = quantity demanded up.**
- A demand curve can be constructed from the individual demands of all consumers in the market.
- **Movements along the demand curve** are due solely to price changes for the product, and are called **changes in quantity demanded**. The demand curve itself does not change position on the graph.

Changes in demand

- When the demand curve **moves position**, it is known as a change in demand. This results from changes in:
  - **taste or fashion** (e.g. clothing, Christmas toys)
  - price of **substitutes** (e.g. branded goods): a price increase for one good increasing the demand for its substitute
  - price of **jointly-demanded products** (e.g. cars and petrol): price changes affect the demand for the joint product
  - **income**: e.g. an increase in disposable income may increase a product's demand because consumers can now afford more
  - **innovation**: new goods and services influence the demand for products currently on the market
  - **population**: Figure 1.3 suggests increasing total demand for products bought by older people and falling demand for those bought by under-16s. Other changes in society affect demand, e.g. (Figure 1.4) a fall in the size of households encourages construction firms to make smaller properties.

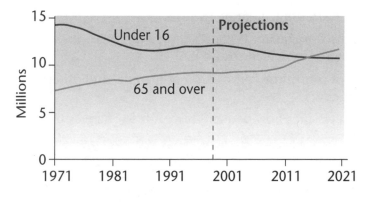

Figure 1.3 UK population
Source: ONS, 1999

Size of household	1961 (%)	1994–5 (%)
1 person	14	27
2 people	30	34
3 people	23	16
4 or more people	33	23
Average size	3.1	2.4

Figure 1.4 Household size, 1961 and 1994–95
Source: OPCS, 1996

(Continued next page)

The markets

Supply

- The fundamental law of supply is: **price up = quantity supplied up; price down = quantity supplied down**.
- Higher prices mean higher profits: more will be supplied as existing firms expand output and/or new firms enter the market.
- **Movements along a supply curve** – expansions or contractions of quantity supplied – occur when the price of the product changes.

Changes in supply

- Changes in **factors of production** also change production costs.
- **Competition**: increased efficiency leads to higher output.
- With **jointly supplied** goods, an increase in the price of one good increases not only its supply, but also that of its joint product.
- **Government involvement**, e.g. taxation and legislation.

Price

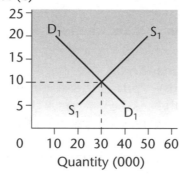

Price (£)

The market, or **equilibrium**, price is when demand equals supply.

Figure 1.5 Equilibrium

Elasticity of demand

- The **price elasticity** of demand measures the responsiveness of the quantity demanded to a change in its price.
- Price elasticity (PED) = $\dfrac{\text{Percentage change in quantity demanded}}{\text{Percentage change in price}}$
- If PED is below 1, demand is **price-inelastic**. When PED is greater than 1, the product is price-sensitive (demand is **price-elastic**).
- PED is affected by availability of substitutes, proportion of income, and other factors, e.g. addiction to the product.
- **Income elasticity** of demand measures how demand responds to changes in consumer incomes.
- **Cross-elasticity** of demand measures how the demand for a good responds to changes in the price of a related good.

Examiner's Tip

Changes in demand and supply are different from changes in quantity demanded and supplied.

AS Business Studies Revision Notes

International trade

Specialisation and exchange

- Specialist firms create mass production, benefiting from **economies of scale** and producing **surpluses** to trade with other countries.
- Influences on specialisation include land/climate, availability of raw materials, and the training and expertise of the workforce.

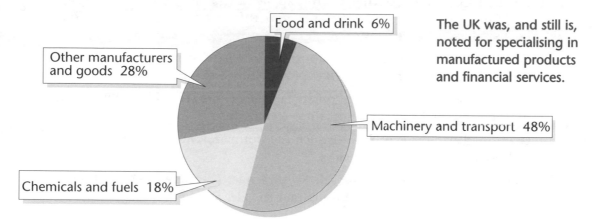

Food and drink 6%

Other manufacturers and goods 28%

The UK was, and still is, noted for specialising in manufactured products and financial services.

Machinery and transport 48%

Chemicals and fuels 18%

Figure 1.6 *UK export of goods, by category, 1998*

Source: ONS, 1999

Free trade and protectionism

- Free trade occurs when the movement of goods and services between countries is not restricted in any way.
- Countries may restrict free trade from taking place, a government using **protectionism** for one or more purposes.

Purpose	Possible approach
improve the country's balance of payments by reducing imports	quotas – physical limits placed on amounts allowed into the country
protect the exchange rate	exchange controls – limit on the amount of foreign currency bought by firms/individuals
raise revenue	tariffs – taxes on imports making them more expensive than home-based goods
safeguard domestic employment and 'infant industries' not yet strong enough to compete with imported competitor products	subsidies – financial support to industries to improve their competitive position

- A government may protect against '**dumping**' of low-priced goods by overseas competitors hoping for market penetration.
- It may also set **embargoes** (no trade in certain items for political or military reasons) or use **procurement** ('buy from within').
- There is **less choice** with protectionism: consumers face higher prices, and inefficiency can result from reduced competition.
- If one country adopts protectionist measures, other countries may follow suit, resulting in a **trade war**.

The European Union (EU)

- The EU has common institutions and common policies on trade, both between members and with the outside world.
- It contains four (the UK, France, Germany and Italy) of the G7 group of industrialised economies, and seven of the world's 12 largest industrial economies.
- The EU's **Common External Tariff** is applied to goods or services entering the EU. This encourages member states to import from other members due to the relative price benefit.
- The **Single Market Act 1986** sought to remove barriers to trade, controls on the flow of capital and abuse of market power.
- EU-wide common standards of quality and safety are set, and UK manufacturers must ensure their products meet these standards.
- Open markets now exist in areas such as information and communications technology, and financial services.
- Free movement of labour is a basic EU principle. There are few formalities or delays in transporting goods throughout the EU.

Other groupings

- The **International Monetary Fund** (IMF) encourages greater co-operation between countries in formulating economic policy.
- The **World Trade Organisation** (WTO) helps trade flow as freely as possible, e.g. by removing tariffs. It is also a forum for trade negotiations and it handles trade disputes.
- **Free trade areas** exist: e.g. **NAFTA**, the North American Free Trade Agreement, when formed in 1994, created the world's largest free trade zone with a population of nearly 400 million.
- **Supplier organisations** are also found: e.g. **OPEC** (Organisation of Petroleum Exporting Countries), established in 1960 to gain some control over oil supply and prices.

Exchange rates

- Importers and exporters find their profit margins are affected by changes in the prices of the currencies they are using.
- A currency's exchange rate shows its **value in other currencies**.
- Under a **floating** exchange rate system, market forces set the rate (price) of the currency on the foreign exchange market.
- Floating exchange rates may encourage **speculators** to gamble on future rate changes, affecting these rates.
- A **fixed rate** system is the alternative, and has often been tried (e.g. the EU's Exchange Rate Mechanism): governments agree the rate at which currencies are exchanged, within set limits.

Examiner's Tip

A fixed exchange rate brings greater certainty to firms trading in overseas markets that profit margins will be maintained.

Progress check

1 Give ONE example of a business in each of the three sectors of the economy.

2 (a) What do these terms mean, and how do they relate to classifying production?
   (i) de-industrialisation;
   (ii) extractive industry;
   (iii) tertiary.

   (b) Give an illustration for each term above.

3 What effect might a cut in direct taxes have on demand levels?

4 Why is a price cut unlikely to benefit a firm with price-inelastic products?

5 Identify THREE effects on a UK firm resulting from the increased mobility of labour within the European Union.

6 If a government introduces tariffs on a range of imported goods, why might demand for these goods remain at the same level?

Answers on page 89

Classification of business

The private and public sectors

- Businesses in the UK are normally grouped into private sector and public sector organisations.

- **Private sector** firms are set up by entrepreneurs who seek to make profit from their business activities.

- Although **controlled** by entrepreneurs, these firms may be owned by different people (or organisations): e.g. companies are owned by shareholders, either as private or institutional (organisation-based) investors.

- The **public sector** consists of those organisations owned and/or financed by central and local **government**.

- This sector provides goods and services to the community through public corporations, local government and other statutory agencies (e.g. the National Health Service).

- The **profit motive is less prominent** here: emphasis is on providing for the community by the community, using funding supplied through taxes and government borrowing.

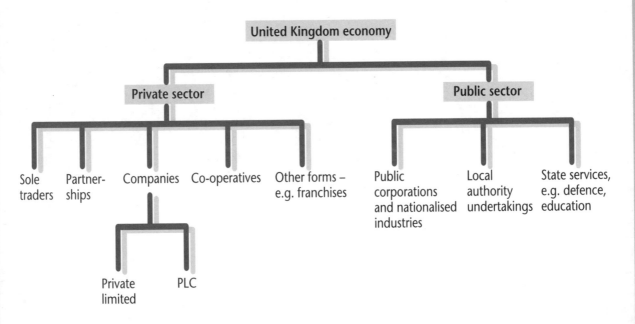

Figure 2.1 Types of organisations in the UK economy

Main features of the private sector

Entrepreneurs and profit

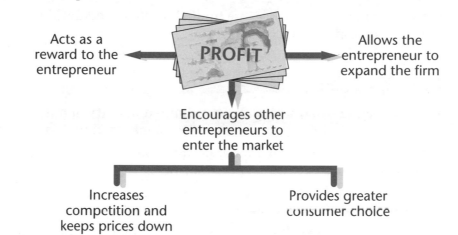

Figure 2.2 Profit

- Profit provides a **measure of success for the business.**

- Prospective lenders use the profit figure to decide whether to lend: potential entrepreneurs check present profit levels in deciding whether to enter the industry.

- Economists view profit as the **reward** of one of the factors of production (enterprise).

- Profit, as the reward for taking risk, is not guaranteed: many firms make losses and close.

- Small profits may be regarded by an entrepreneur as poor reward for risk-taking: the firm's **profitability** is too low.

- This results in **continual change** in the private sector.

Industry	Registrations (000)	De-registrations (000)
Agriculture, fishing, mining, energy	4.1	6.0
Manufacturing	12.6	14.9
Construction	18.4	17.4
Hotels, catering	16.8	16.3
Transport	9.3	8.2
Finance and business services	68.7	36.0

Figure 2.3 Enterprises registering and de-registering by industry, 1998
Source: DTI SME Statistics Unit

- Figure 2.3 illustrates the move from the primary and secondary sectors to the tertiary sector.

- Compared with 1997, registrations fell in agriculture/fishing (600) and manufacturing (900) in 1998, whereas de-registrations in these areas both rose by 100: the net result was a loss of some 4000 businesses. This compares with a net gain of nearly 33 000 service businesses, which grew by over 100 000 in the five years to 1998 to 1 in 4 of all VAT-registered UK firms.

(Continued next page)

Main features of the private sector

Legal liability and legal status

- Most commercial companies are **limited by share** and must include 'limited' or 'plc' as appropriate in their name.
- This warns those trading with such a company that any debts it incurs from trading may not be recoverable due to the limited liability of its owners (shareholders).
- Sole traders and partnerships have **unlimited liability**: if business debts cannot be met by the firm's resources, the owner(s) may be forced to sell personal assets.
- Where a limited company cannot pay its debts from its own resources, it cannot make the owners use their personal finances.
- Limited liability encourages **greater investment** to take place, and ensures a demand for stocks and shares.
- Another important difference between these forms of business ownership is in their **legal status**.
- Limited companies are **incorporated** bodies, having a **separate legal existence** from their shareholders.
- Sole traders and partnerships are **unincorporated** businesses, and do not have this separate legal existence.

Corporate objectives

- A company's **mission statement** shows its overall aim. This is then translated into **corporate objectives**.
- Corporate objectives are developed into **functional** ones, which are then expanded into **individual** objectives for employees to achieve.
- Achievement is measured through appraising individuals and by adopting a **management by objectives** approach.

Corporate objective	Value to the firm
Increase market share and become the market leader	Greater control over market price; easier to get new products accepted
Maximise profits	Pleases shareholders and improves share price
Ensure long-term growth and stability	Economies of scale; helps protect the company from being taken over
Stay a market leader through technological innovation	Remain competitive in the market
Diversify in order to develop new markets	Exploit profitable markets; spread the risk by operating in different markets

- Objectives will change over time, and their relative importance will vary according to the influence of the different stakeholders.

Examiner's Tip

Individuals seek to make profit as entrepreneurs: the **profit motive** is the foundation of the private sector.

Sole traders

- A sole trader business exists when, even though there may be a number of employees, there is only **one** owner.
- The sole trader form of ownership tends to occur where **personal services** are provided, **little capital** is needed to start up, and large-scale production is not relevant.

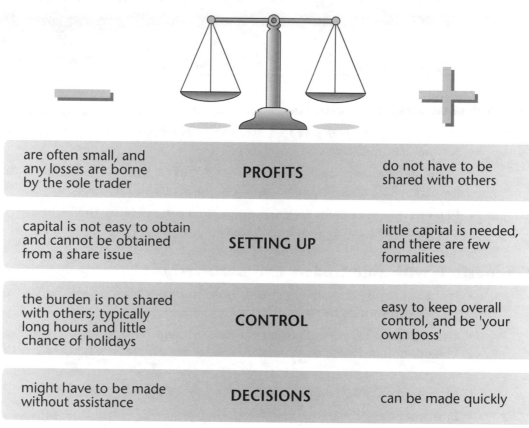

are often small, and any losses are borne by the sole trader	**PROFITS**	do not have to be shared with others
capital is not easy to obtain and cannot be obtained from a share issue	**SETTING UP**	little capital is needed, and there are few formalities
the burden is not shared with others; typically long hours and little chance of holidays	**CONTROL**	easy to keep overall control, and be 'your own boss'
might have to be made without assistance	**DECISIONS**	can be made quickly

Figure 2.4 *Features of the sole trader*

Partnerships

- These are also unincorporated, associated with professions (e.g. accountants, lawyers) where capital outlay is small.
- Other similarities with sole traders are that they are simple to establish, their financial affairs can be kept private, and the owners still face unlimited liability.
- Partners draw up a **written agreement** on the rights and duties of individual partners.
- The rules laid down in the **1890 Partnership Act** apply where there is no agreement.
  - Profits and losses are shared equally.
  - Partners' loans receive 5% interest per annum.
  - Each has an equal say in how the firm operates.
- If a sole trader is thinking of converting to a partnership, the key issues to consider are:

(Continued next page)

Legal structure in the private sector

Benefits	Drawbacks
specialisation can take place (each partner can specialise in a different business function)	**decision-making may take longer** (the new partner must be consulted)
additional skills may also be introduced by the new partner	if/when the new partner dies or leaves, a **new partnership** must be created
more capital is available (an extra owner is an extra investor)	the **profit must be shared** between the partners
expansion is therefore easier	**control** of the business must also be shared

Limited companies

- A limited company is **private** (Ltd) unless its memorandum of association states it is public limited (PLC).
- A private company cannot advertise its shares for sale to the public or through the Stock Exchange: its share capital must not exceed £50 000.
- PLCs have a minimum £50 000 capital, and can sell their shares to the public and be quoted on the Stock Exchange.

Comparison with sole traders and partnerships

- Limited liability encourages greater **investment**, leading to greater size and greater **economies of scale**.
- Through its separate legal existence, the company owns assets, takes legal action in its own name, and does not face continuity problems when owners die or retire.
- More formality and expense is necessary to set up.
- Business affairs are less private.
- Greater size may result in diseconomies of scale.
- Ownership of PLCs can be transferred (via the Stock Exchange) against the wishes of the directors.
- Shareholders may vote for short-term policies to make short-term profits, leading to greater instability.

'Divorce of ownership and control'

- Shareholders **own** a company but do not **control** it.
- Through the **Annual General Meeting**, shareholders appoint specialist directors to exercise control on their behalf.
- Once ownership and control is separated, decisions made by the directors – the controllers – may clash with the wishes of (some of) the shareholders – the owners.

Examiner's Tip

PLCs are usually larger than private companies, and find ownership and control more clearly separated.

Other private sector structures

Franchises

- These businesses use the **name and logo of an existing company**.
- Franchising is a major growth area in the UK economy: by the end of 1999 there were nearly 600 business format franchises, comprising almost 30 000 franchisees employing nearly a quarter of a million people.
- Examples include **The Body Shop, Thornton's Confectionery, Prontaprint Ltd** and **ANC** package delivery service.

> Franchisees need the use of a car, a telephone, a reasonable size room at home (or use of the garage), plus plenty of energy and determination. Card Connection will provide everything else needed to make the business a success.
>
> *Source: Card Connection, 1999*
>
> McDonald's has always been a franchising company and has relied on our franchisees to play a major role in our success.
>
> *Source: McDonald's, 1999*

- The **franchisee** buys the franchise, contracting with and paying a fee to the **franchisor** (the company). Typically:

The franchisee	The franchisor
agrees to follow set rules, e.g. layout of premises and product standards	supplies the decor and assists with layout
buys only from the franchisor or other named supplier	allows the franchisee to use the product and the logo

- The **British Franchise Association**, a non-profitmaking body, regulates franchising in the UK.
- Types of franchise agreements include:
  - **manufacturer-retailer** (some petrol stations and car dealers)
  - **wholesaler-retailer** (Spar and other voluntary groups)
  - **trademark-retailer** ('fast food' outlets).

Benefits for both parties

- The franchisor can **expand** without making a large capital investment, since the franchisee provides the capital.
- The company knows that its franchisees, who are not on a salary, will be highly **motivated** by the direct financial incentive to make their franchise a financial success.
- The franchisee gains a **recognised product** backed by successful business methods, and receives **expert support**: success is therefore more likely than for an 'independent' entrepreneur.

(Continued next page)

Other private sector structures

Co-operatives

- Although the larger UK co-operatives operate as limited companies, owning capital is not the dominant factor in the co-operative movement. Most co-operative societies exist to provide a **service** for their member-owners and for the public.

- **Control** is shared democratically, each member having a single vote: trading surpluses may be distributed to members in proportion to their trade with the society.

- **Consumer co-operatives**, where customers collectively own the business, are found in Europe and Japan: in the UK these include housing co-operatives and credit unions (formed to allow people to benefit from collective saving and borrowing).

- There are over 4000 local **co-operative retail societies** (CRS) – the 'Co-ops' – in the UK. Many of their products come from the **Co-operative Wholesale Society Ltd** (CWS): its role is to buy in bulk and to supply the retail co-ops with its own (about 3000 own-brand) goods.

- The CWS is also the UK's largest farmer. Other co-operative activities include banking and insurance.

- The **Co-operative Retail Trading Group** (CRTG) links individual retail co-operatives. By 1999 the CRTG accounted for over 90% of co-operative food buying power.

- There are over 1000 UK-based **producer** (**worker**) **co-operatives**, many existing previously in a different ownership form: printing, publishing, fashion/textiles and agriculture are popular areas.

- ICOM, the federation of worker co-operatives, was formed in 1971 and supports its members by providing training and business advice: local **Co-operative Development Agencies** also support these worker co-operatives.

Mutuality

- Some building societies and life assurance firms are **non-profitmaking** organisations, existing for the benefit of their members (customers).

- In the 1990s, many changed status (e.g. the **Halifax** converted from a building society to a bank, becoming a limited company), producing cash 'windfalls' for the existing members, many of whom became shareholders.

Measures of size

Turnover

- The **annual sales** indicate a firm's ability to obtain finance and to benefit from economies of scale.
- However, turnover can vary greatly from year to year, and does not automatically indicate market value or profit levels.

Capital employed

- Capital employed (or 'net assets') shows **net investment** and is compared with profit to measure profitability.
- It can be a difficult figure to measure because firms in the same industry may use different bases for valuing their assets.

Profits

- A firm's profit figure may be used to indicate its size.
- One drawback of using this measure is that different firms in the same industry will operate on **different profit margins**.

Employees

- This can be a good indicator to use, but firms in different industries have **differing capital/labour ratios**: e.g. a service firm is normally more labour-intensive than a manufacturer.

Profits before tax		Turnover		MANUFACTURERS Delta Glynwed	Capital employed		Employees	
£ million		£ million			£ million			
(1) Delta	40.3	(1) Glynwed	1015		(1) Glynwed	334.5	(1) Delta	15 383
(2) Glynwed	36.4	(2) Delta	663		(2) Delta	315.3	(2) Glynwed	11 624
				RETAILERS Tesco Sainsbury's				
(1) Tesco	842	(1) Tesco	17 158		(1) Sainsbury	4663	(1) Sainsbury	177 906
(2) Sainsbury	832	(2) Sainsbury	15 196		(2) Tesco	4377	(2) Tesco	172 712

Figure 2.5 *Comparisons of size*
Source: annual accounts of Glynwed plc and Delta plc (1998), and | Sainsbury plc and Tesco plc (1999)

Examiner's Tip

Firms in the same industry should be compared using the same indicator of size.

Public ownership

Public corporations, nationalisation and privatisation

- Public corporations have a **separate legal existence** through the Act of Parliament creating them.
- Their assets are state-owned on behalf of the community.
- Their objectives, whilst influenced by commercial considerations, often emphasise **social aspects**.
- They normally have **financial targets** to achieve, such as a target return on capital employed.
- A public corporation is **controlled** through:
  - its government minister and a board
  - a consumer council protecting consumer interests
  - being audited by the Competition Commission.
- **Nationalisation** takes an industry into public ownership.
- Nationalised industries came to be seen as inefficient and over-subsidised **monopolies** which lacked competition.
- The government's response was to privatise – return to private ownership – most nationalised industries.
- Recent privatisation in the UK includes:

1979 BP	1984 Sealink
1981 British Sugar	1988 British Steel, Rover
1983 Forestry Commission	1990 Electricity supply/generation

- **Deregulation** has also been used by the UK government (and the EU) to stimulate competition, e.g. in broadcasting.
- Critics of privatisation argue that privatising 'natural monopoly' industries may mean **losing economies of scale**.
- Private monopolies are likely to be **less well regulated** than public sector ones.

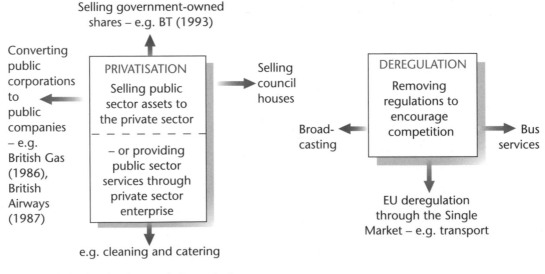

Figure 2.6 *Privatisation and deregulation*

Examiner's Tip

Privatisation has brought with it drawbacks as well as benefits: thus the need for 'watchdogs' such as Oftel.

Progress check

1 State TWO reasons why profit is important to an entrepreneur.

2 What is the main difference between an incorporated and an unincorporated business?

3 Name THREE occupations where sole traders are commonly found.

4 State TWO reasons why sole traders may choose to convert their businesses into limited companies rather than partnerships.

5 Identify TWO differences between a franchisee and a sole trader.

6 What forms of co-operative exist in the UK?

7 Identify THREE differences between a public corporation and a PLC.

8 Give TWO disadvantages to a consumer when buying from a monopoly.

Answers on pages 89–90

External and other influences

The business cycle

Stage	Firms
Recession: contracting output; gloomy outlook	experience falling demand and so cut prices and dismiss staff; losses are made; investment falls; some go out of business
Recovery: the economy starts expanding: rising, but limited, expectations	experience increase in demand; review their employment and investment positions but still lack confidence
Boom: rapid growth in output; high confidence but fear of inflation	invest and take on staff; may find skill shortages; increase prices and profit margins; utilise spare capacity
Downturn (recession): growth slows again	experience falling demand and profits; start reducing output and investment

Figure 3.1 Stages in the business cycle

The effect on firms

- In the cycle, personal consumption normally fluctuates less than business investment. This affects firms in different ways when a recession or **slump** – a time of falling real incomes – occurs:

  - firms producing capital equipment (machinery, etc.) will be badly affected by the reduced investment of other firms

  - those making and selling consumer durables are badly hit if consumers postpone replacing these until an economic upturn occurs, when confidence about employment and income rises

  - firms making and selling basic necessities will experience less of a fall in demand – it may increase, as consumers switch expenditure away from luxuries onto these items.

- Firms that have **diversified** are in a stronger position to survive.

Examiner's Tip

By surviving a recession, firms have examined and overcome weaknesses in their product range, expertise, and organisation.

Interest and exchange rates

Interest rates

- Interest rates indicate the **cost of borrowing money**.

- Interest rates and borrowing decisions are influenced by **opportunity cost**: for the borrower this is the cost of not taking out the loan (i.e. going without the item bought by the loan) and for the lender it is not having the cash to spend.

UK interest rates

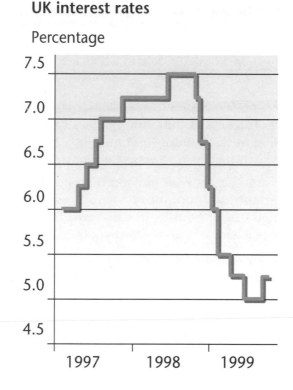

If interest rates are increased, borrowing – and so spending – will fall, taking demand-led pressure out of the economy and reducing inflation. Firms face not only the direct cost of increased interest payments, but also a falling demand for their goods and services.

Figure 3.2 UK interest rates, 1997–1999

Exchange rates

- Chapter 1 explained exchange rates. Fluctuating exchange rates cause problems for importers and exporters, and may discourage entrepreneurs from establishing overseas markets.

- A **rising exchange rate** means cheaper imported items for importers but, for exporters, lower price-competitiveness and profits.

- Therefore, exporters gain and importers lose from **falling rates**.

- **Multinationals** are in a stronger position to cope with these fluctuations, because they can move resources from country to country to take advantage of these fluctuations.

> ### Examiner's Tip
> The level of interest rates is important for firms and individuals, which is why governments use them as a key tool of economic policy.

Unemployment and inflation

Unemployment

- **Full employment** is a typical key government objective (although there are various ways of interpreting what is meant by 'full').
- Unemployment rates vary considerably across the UK: areas that used to rely on heavy industries and which have since declined often have some of the highest rates of unemployment.
- For example, Cleveland and Merseyside were traditionally strong shipbuilding areas before this industry experienced a decline, and South Yorkshire was a prosperous coalmining region. By Spring 1998 these areas had unemployment rates well above the UK average, at 7.3%, 10.9% and 9.6%, respectively (source: ONS, 1999).
- Unemployment can be:
  - **structural** – industries face structural decline through lack of competitiveness: e.g. the old 'staple' industries of shipbuilding and mining. This has affected these areas, and continues with the trend towards de-industrialisation
  - **frictional** – caused by the time lag between moving from one job to another. It is linked to labour's **geographical immobility** where a person will not move to another area (e.g. the high cost of housing in south-east England), and its **occupational immobility** (e.g. lack of skill to do the jobs available)
  - **casual** or **seasonal** – found in sectors such as agriculture and tourism
  - **cyclical** – due to a downturn in the business cycle.

What is inflation?

- Inflation is **a persistent tendency for prices to rise over time**.
- Because of the effect of inflation on firms and people, its **control** becomes a key government objective.

Causes of inflation

- **Cost–push** inflation occurs when production costs increase, e.g. due to pay rises not being supported by productivity increases, or through costs of imported items rising due to the pound falling on the foreign exchange market.
- **Demand–pull** inflation occurs when aggregate (total) demand in the economy exceeds aggregate supply.
- Governments attempt to control demand–pull inflation by **monetary policy** – reducing the availability or increasing the cost of credit – and **fiscal policy** – increasing taxation to reduce spending power or cutting government spending to reduce demand.
- **Deflation** occurs when this downward pressure on economic activity produces falling demand and prices: the danger is that, as a result, firms reduce output and employment.

Measuring inflation

- A popular measure of inflation is the **retail prices index** (RPI).

- The prices of a representative sample of purchases made by households – the average 'shopping basket' – are weighted in importance and recorded.

- Other measures of inflation include the 'factory gate' indicator of the price of firms' inputs.

- These indicators have their limitations. For example, the RPI is based on the average shopping basket: but many people who rely on RPI figures for increases in their income may have quite different spending patterns, with their increased costs not reflecting those shown by RPI calculations.

The effect of inflation

- Entrepreneurs have **inflationary expectations**: plans are influenced by what they expect to happen to inflation in the future.

- The actions taken as a result may help fulfil these expectations: e.g. if the rate of inflation is expected to increase, entrepreneurs may buy goods now, increasing present demand levels and reinforcing any demand–pull inflation. Their employees may seek higher wage increases on the basis of the expected rise in inflation, increasing costs and adding to any cost–push inflation in the economy.

- Inflation affects **firms' behaviour and chances of survival**
  - long-term planning becomes more difficult
  - profit margins may be squeezed, since firms cannot pass increased costs on (since their selling prices become uncompetitive)
  - the increase in interest rates during inflationary periods hits firms with high debt borrowing and may encourage them to pay higher dividends (which reduces their cash levels)
  - UK exporters may find the increase in their prices due to inflation makes them uncompetitive overseas.

- Inflation also hits those on a fixed income such as pensioners – though indexing of pensions may counter this – and will therefore **affect the demand level** for firms supplying these consumers.

- It may also **distort general economic behaviour** (high inflation often encourages saving and reduces spending, leading to an economic downturn. Low inflation tends to encourage spending and fuels output and recovery).

- **Firms may benefit** from inflation: e.g. those with high borrowing find that the sum owed is falling in real terms.

- The action of firms can also **counter inflation**: e.g. where cut-throat competition occurs, such as the 'price war' amongst supermarkets in 1999 triggered by Wal-Mart's takeover of Asda.

Examiner's Tip

The UK government uses inflation targeting: a target inflation level is set, the Monetary Policy Committee (MPC) manipulating interest rates to meet it.

Government support

Areas of influence

- Local and central government, together with the European Union, influence a firm's decisions regarding its:
  - **location**: e.g. granting planning permission
  - **workforce**: e.g. passing health and safety legislation
  - **trade links**: e.g. removing tariff barriers
  - **expansion**: e.g. legislation controlling monopolies
  - **income**: e.g. altering tax rates
  - **finance**: e.g. influencing the level of interest rates.
- The UK government (and the EU) has economic objectives to control inflation, keep balance of payments stable and unemployment low.
- The government also tries to make its economy compete successfully with other competitor economies in the global marketplace.

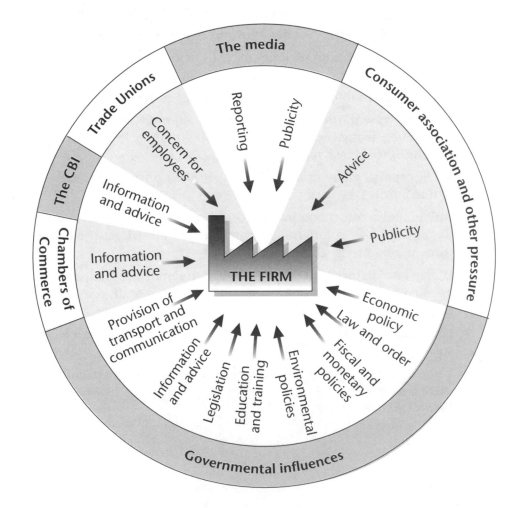

Figure 3.3 *External influences on a firm*

Examples of UK government involvement

- The **Department of Trade and Industry** (DTI) supports UK industry in many ways: e.g. through its **Business Link** support network.

- The **Office for National Statistics** (ONS) is the government agency responsible for compiling many of the UK's economic and social statistics, used by firms to analyse market and other trends. Its publications include *Regional Trends* and *Social Trends*.

- The **Export Credit Guarantee Department** (ECGD) supports exports by providing guarantees and insurance against loss. It covers around £3 billion of UK exports each year.

- The **Department for Education and Employment** operates the 'New Deal' training scheme, which provides financial support for salary and training costs.

Regional policy

- The UK government and the EU seek to correct economic imbalances between areas by stimulating the economy in less well-off areas.

- This reduces inequality of income, helps firms in these areas compete more effectively, and counters unemployment problems due to structural decline and geographical immobility of labour.

- The UK government has offered selective regional financial assistance, e.g. by encouraging firms to settle in development areas (an approach reinforced by the EU's Regional Policy).

- **Enterprise zones** were set up in areas hit by severe unemployment, and received government grants.

- **Assisted areas** have been established, with the government offering grants to firms to settle there.

The European Union (EU)

- The EU supports national and local government initiatives.

- Regional financial support is given through the **European Regional Development Fund**, and financial support for training initiatives through the **European Social Fund**.

- The launch of the Single Market programme in 1985 led to the creation of the **Social Charter**, signed by 11 governments (excluding the UK at the time) in 1989.

- The Single Market is the greatest assistance given to competitive firms by the EU. The objective – to remove trade barriers and allow free access to markets – means that companies have access to a market with a spending power even larger than that of North America.

EXTERNAL AND OTHER INFLUENCES

Legal influences

General principles

- The UK parliament passes 'home' legislation.

- In the EU, **Regulations** apply directly in all member states and do not have to be confirmed by national parliaments to be legally binding: if there is conflict between a Regulation and existing national law, the Regulation prevails.

- EU **Directives** bind member states, but leave the method of implementation up to national governments.

Consumer protection

- Consumers enter **contracts** when buying goods or services. To support contract law, UK governments and the EU have a range of consumer protection laws.

- In the UK, the **Sale and Supply of Goods Act (1994)** consolidated other Acts relating to selling goods. Under this Act, goods must be of **satisfactory quality**, i.e. fit to be sold. They must also be fit for their intended purpose and – if sold by description – they must match their description.

- The **Trade Descriptions Acts (1968 and 1972)** make it illegal to give a false oral or written description of a good or service.

- The **Consumer Credit Act (1974)** protects consumers against signing unfair contracts and requires firms to state interest rates.

- The **Financial Services Act (1986)** ensures that firms lending money or offering financial services are controlled.

- The **Food Safety Act (1990)** consolidates law on the supply of food products and protects consumers from being sold unfit food.

- The **Weights and Measures Acts (to 1985)** protect consumers by making it an offence to sell goods underweight or under quantity.

The Office of Fair Trading (OFT)

- Established in 1973, the OFT helps to protect the economic welfare of consumers, and enforces UK competition policy. Its roles are to:
  - put right any trading practices against consumer interests
  - regulate the provision of consumer credit
  - investigate anti-competitive practices
  - help establish market structures encouraging competition.

EU influences

- EU Directives seek to establish **common levels of consumer protection** throughout the Union.

- Some Directives have removed trade barriers, others concentrate on transport arrangements to ensure free movement of goods, while the 'New Approach Directives' control product design and give a 'level playing field' for product safety requirements across the EU.

- Examples of EU consumer legislation Directives include **Foodstuff Prices**, **Misleading Advertising**, **Toy Safety** and **Package Travel**.

Education and consumer information	Consumer requirements	Protection of consumers' interests
Product packaging: e.g. – pre-packaged products – quick-frozen foods *Product labelling:* e.g. – household appliances – beverages – footwear – tobacco *Special indications:* e.g. – designation of origin *Price indications:* e.g. – foodstuffs – gas and electricity *Advertising:* e.g. – misleading adverts – advertising medicines	*Product safety:* e.g. – general product safety – toy safety – dangerous imitations *Consumer health:* e.g. – food safety – veterinary inspections – genetic modification *Quality of goods and services:* e.g. – cosmetic products – foodstuff quality – quality of the environment	*Electronic commerce:* e.g. – legal aspects *Contracts:* e.g. – contracts away from business premises – unfair contract terms – guarantees *Transport:* e.g. – package travel – air transport *Financial and insurance services:* e.q. – electronic payments – consumer credit *Legal redress:* e.g. – access to justice

Figure 3.4 The general framework for EU activities in favour of the consumer

The influence of consumer legislation on business

- Protection – e.g. against exploiting a firm's trade name
- Costs – e.g. food safety laws creating hygiene-related costs
- Customer satisfaction – by meeting customer expectations as well as legal requirements, products are more saleable
- Internal systems – e.g. firms seek to improve Quality Control, and continue developing a 'quality culture'.

Competition policy

- Monopolies and anti-competitive practices are deemed to be against the public interest.
- The EU's Merger Control Regulation (1990) stops mergers that lead to or strengthen dominant market position or impede competition.
- The use of subsidies by member states for their industries is also controlled by the EU, to prevent free trade becoming distorted.
- In the UK, privatised companies are regulated, e.g. Oftel and Ofgas, and the Competition Commission investigates mergers.
- Monopolies, mergers and restrictive trade practices fall under the 1973 Fair Trading Act: anti-competitive practices are covered by the 1980 Competition Act.

Examiner's Tip

Legislation has a two-fold effect on business: it acts as a constraint on firms, and as a framework within which firms operate.

Demographic influences

Key trends

- The UK has experienced both net immigration and net emigration, but the effect on skill levels is more important than the total numbers involved. The removal of barriers to the **free movement of labour** in the EU is a major influence on labour migration levels.

- Internally, the distribution of the workforce also affects firms' planning: recent trends include firms moving to the south-east.

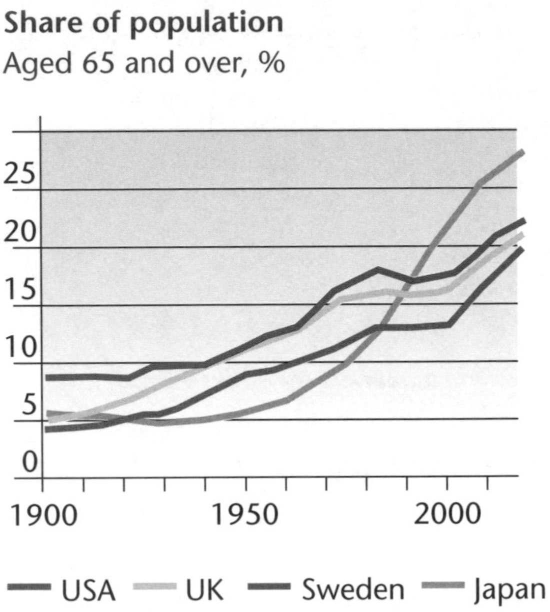

Share of population
Aged 65 and over, %

Figure 3.5 Share of population aged 65 and over (%)
Source: National Institute of Population and Social Security Research

- The average age of the UK's population is increasing. Effects on firms include changing demand levels for age-related goods and services, and pressure from the state for additional tax and other contributions to support the ageing population.

- **Part-time work** has grown in importance: employers gain from increased flexibility, but now often have to provide the same conditions of employment for part-timers, which increases costs.

- **'Flexitime'** has increased: employee morale improves through adapting work to fit personal needs, but employers have to ensure that a 'core' of staff will be available during key periods.

- **Fixed-term employment** contracts are found: they give an employer greater control over labour costs.

Examiner's Tip

The labour market is becoming increasingly flexible, with two workers in five at present outside permanent employment.

Other influences

Social responsibilities

- Modern-day organisations are aware of the importance of their image, and acknowledge their social responsibilities to: **employees**, **customers**, **shareholders** and **other stakeholders**.

- Examples of specific social responsibilities include:

  - **equal opportunities** – as well as obeying legislation, firms will wish to publicise their commitment to EO

  - **ethical trading** – firms balance moral and ethical stances with the need to make an adequate return on investment

  - **environmental awareness** – firms realise the negative effect of bad publicity

  - **health and safety** – firms understand that a good health and safety record creates a positive image.

An example of social responsibility

- These extracts from Marks & Spencer plc's 1999 annual review explain how social responsibility can bring commercial benefits.

Equal opportunities Both our employees and our customers reflect the diversity of the communities served by Marks & Spencer. We therefore extend our commitment to equal opportunities beyond our employment practices to the ways we welcome customers to our stores. New training is helping staff to understand the specific needs of people from ethnic minority groups or those with disabilities. This also supports our commercial objective of responding to every group within the complex modern marketplace.

Health and Safety Our investment in training many of our store safety officers towards an NVQ in health and safety is paying off for staff and organisation alike. Overall safety standards have risen even higher, meaning less time and money is lost through accident or ill health. We are also partnering public authorities in agreeing common safety standards for our buildings. This too brings business benefits, by speeding up local planning procedures for our widely located property base.

Ethical trading Agreeing good working standards has always been important to our partnership with suppliers. This presents more of a challenge now that our global supply base has become so vast and complex. But we are determined to do what we can. So we have joined the Ethical Trading Initiative and are enforcing a set of Global Sourcing Principles. These cover areas such as workforce rights, accurate labelling of country of origin and environmental responsibility.

Environmental advance Each year we become more sophisticated in minimising the environmental impact of our operations. During 1998 we were the first UK retailer to test an advanced software system called 'Greencode'. Managers at our Leicester store used this system to co-ordinate the building's heating, lighting, transport, waste disposal and other activities to cut waste and minimise its overall impact on the surrounding environment. This trial is enabling us to consider implementing this system more widely across our stores.

Pressure groups

- These are **organised groups** of people with **similar interests**, who attempt to **influence others**, notably government and industries.

- They range in size from international organisations such as **Greenpeace** and **Amnesty International**, to small community groups concerned only with local matters.

- A pressure group's success largely depends on the level of financial, public and political support, as well as on the organisational ability of the group itself.

- **Sector groups** (e.g. British Medical Association, RAC and AA) represent a particular section; **cause groups** (e.g. ASH – Action on Smoking and Health) promote a particular cause.

- Pressure groups affect firms: for example, trade unions act on behalf of their members, and the AA and RAC influence vehicle manufacturers on issues such as safety and fuel economy.

- **The media** also influence firms, affecting **costs** (e.g. having to correct faulty products) and **sales** (by good or bad publicity).

Technological influences

- Certain industries have been revolutionised by technology: e.g. the financial sector's use of electronic funds transfer, telephone banking and e-banking, and manufacturers using CAD/CAM equipment.

- Many high-street firms now offer internet-based shopping. This 'e-commerce' gives 24-hour access, allows customers in other countries access to the firm's products, and can cut costs.

- An EU Directive which creates a consistent legal framework for e-commerce from 2000 should reinforce this growth.

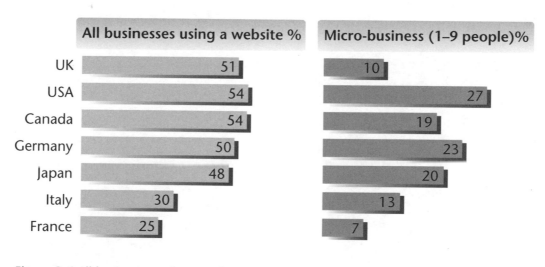

	All businesses using a website %	Micro-business (1–9 people)%
UK	51	10
USA	54	27
Canada	54	19
Germany	50	23
Japan	48	20
Italy	30	13
France	25	7

Figure 3.6 *All businesses using a website.*

Source: e-commerce@its.best.co.uk 1999

Examiner's Tip

Benefits from technological advances include lower costs, greater speed of production and sale, and improved customer satisfaction.

EXTERNAL AND OTHER INFLUENCES

Progress check

1 Distinguish between interest and exchange rates.

2 What is the difference between cost–push and demand–pull inflation?

3 Why do governments try to support industry?

4 In what ways can a firm benefit from government assistance?

5 What effect does consumer protection law have on firms?

6 Why does the UK legislate against anti-competitive practices?

7 Illustrate how a firm's ethical policy may clash with its need to make profits.

Answers on page 90

Structure and efficiency

Internal organisation

Forms of organisational structure

- Most UK organisations were historically organised by internal business functions/departments – Personnel, Accounts, etc.

- This form of corporate culture is often called **role culture**, and the formal, traditional organisational system based on these departments/functions is called **line organisation**.

- The advantage of this organisational structure is that **roles and responsibilities are well-defined** with a **clear chain of command**.

- A line structure tends to be **bureaucratic** in nature, with a narrow span of control due to the many layers of hierarchy.

- As they grow, firms rely more on **specialist** support functions. A **line and staff organisation** recognises these specialists.

> Organised into five core businesses ... Shell companies operate independently, although they draw on a common network of service companies ... The service companies provide a range of specialist advice and resources ...
>
> *Source:* Shell's Energy *(extract), Royal Dutch/Shell Group of Companies, 1999*

- **Organisation charts** show the formal structure of these firms: their hierarchy, degree of specialisation, and roles. They date quickly, however, and do not show informal structures.

- Today, many organisations have reduced the number of layers in their hierarchy, restructuring to take the emphasis away from functions and towards **operations**, **projects**, or **tasks**. This is called a **matrix structure**.

- The matrix structure combines the use of line departments with project (task) teams drawn from the various line functions.

- It is effective in firms with **wide spans of control** and few **hierarchical levels** of responsibility. These firms are often in **fast-changing markets**, selling products with relatively **short life-cycles** (e.g. telecommunications).

- Traditional departmental barriers are broken down and motivation is increased through varied work (e.g. moving to a new team/task), but overall control is more complex, and some team members may face a clash of loyalties between the task and their department.

Examiner's Tip

Management achieves **planning, control** and **co-ordination** by operating within a suitable organisational structure.

Principles of management structure

Delayering

- Delayering **removes one or more layers** of the firm's management hierarchy. It may be implemented to increase spans of control, or to reduce communication problems and related costs.
- A side-effect may be extra pressure and stress on staff involved.

> Following his appointment, Manfred Halper implemented a programme to restructure the plumbing business for growth. These changes have eliminated an entire layer of management and made the business more market and consumer focused, as well as removing unnecessary costs and duplication.
>
> *Source: Delta plc annual report and accounts 1998 (extract)*

Span of control

- This can be defined as the **number of subordinates directly under the control of a manager.**
- It is described as **wide** when the manager has many subordinates, and **narrow** when the manager has few subordinates.
- The width of an individual's span of control is influenced by:
  - the degree of **complexity** of the work involved
  - the level of staff **skill and ability**
  - the **manager's own level** of ability and training.
- By widening the span of control, **delegation** is encouraged, and **fewer layers of hierarchy** are now required, improving speed of communication between top and bottom of the hierarchy.
- By narrowing the span of control, there may be **less pressure** on employees; **closer management supervision** is possible, important in certain industries (e.g. where safety is at a premium).
- Too narrow a span leads to over-supervision, denying staff the chance to show initiative: too wide a span means lack of control and the chance of costly mistakes.

Chain of command

- This establishes how **power** and **control** flow through a firm.
- The chain becomes more complicated as size increases: whereas a sole trader may liaise with all employees, large companies have chains of command that go through a number of layers of authority.
- Organisational structures can be **tall** or **flat**.
- Tall structures indicate **long chains of command**. As a result:
  - decisions take time to reach employees lower down the chain
  - this can lead to a 'them and us' feeling of remoteness
  - spans of control are often narrow
  - employees are usually highly task-specialised.
- Flat structures are increasingly popular, and are associated with **smaller organisations** and **shorter chains of command**.

Centralisation

- Centralisation allows managers to make and communicate quickly decisions which are consistent across the organisation.

- However, a centralised structure denies those lower down the chain of command the power or authority to make their own decisions.

- As an illustration, many well-known 'fast food' outlets operating as franchises have little if any scope regarding display, pricing policy and the style or amount of advertising.

> Marks & Spencer has outgrown the highly centralised structure which drove much of our past expansion and success. While retaining the efficiencies and scale of a large organisation, we are radically restructuring our business to become more responsive to the needs of our customer.
>
> *Source: Marks & Spencer plc annual review 1999 (extract)*

- **Decentralised** structures are increasingly popular. Associated with greater authority at 'unit' (e.g. shop) level, they:
  - allow a more effective **local response** to local needs
  - improve employee **motivation** through greater involvement in decision-making
  - lead to more effective **management by objectives (MBO)** through personally-devised objectives being set
  - lead to **management by exception** by more accurate budgeting and an improved control system through the use of variances.

Delegation

- A manager may delegate certain powers to subordinates.

- The key to successful delegation is **mutual trust**.

- If employees are to carry out delegated tasks, they must accept **responsibility** for carrying out the tasks, and for any failure.

- The employee who will carry out the delegated work must be given the **authority** to do so: this must be communicated to others.

- Delegation results in the subordinate being **accountable** to the manager – and, in turn, the manager to the next person up the chain of command – for the success of the work.

- A side-benefit of delegation is that the junior employee takes on extra responsibility, and is being **trained for later advancement**.

- Delegation may be unsuccessful, where the work delegated is **unsuitable** (e.g. too complex), the delegator may have **difficulty in delegating** due to unwillingness to relinquish tasks, or the subordinate may **lack adequate training, confidence or motivation**.

Examiner's Tip

Delegation is associated with larger organisations, because no one person can effectively control all the functions of a large firm.

Communication in the organisation

The role of business communication

- Business communication transmits information through the hierarchy/chain of command using communication channels.
- The **formal channels** are indicated by the firm's formal structure, shown by the vertical chains of command in its organisation chart.
- **Horizontal** communication channels also exist: e.g. communication at team meetings where the team is drawn from several departments.
- A channel may be '**open**' to all in the firm, e.g. a noticeboard, or '**closed**', limited to named individuals or roles.
- **Informal** communication channels co-exist with formal ones. They can assume great importance in firms with **tall structures**, and where the formal channels are not working efficiently.
- Most managers recognise the value of informal channels due to their typically **positive effect on employee morale** and motivation.
- **Oral communication** is most valuable for transmitting basic, low-volume information quickly. It may be informal (e.g. a telephone call) or formal, such as in a business meeting or an interview.
- **Written communication** is widely used where high-volume and/or technical information needs transmitting, and has the advantage that a record of the communication is available if required.

Barriers to effective communication

- The **transmitter**:
  - uses inappropriate or inaccurate language
  - omits important information.
- The **message**:
  - is sent using inappropriate methods
  - goes through an over-long chain of command
  - contains a high level of irrelevant information.
- The **medium**:
  - is unsuitable for the information being transmitted
  - is too slow in getting the message to the recipient.
- The **recipient**:
  - may choose to ignore the message
  - is in an unsuitable physical/emotional state to receive it
  - interprets the message incorrectly.

Overcoming the barriers

- **Staff training** in communication procedures needs reviewing; communication **media** need evaluating for clarity and suitability; and the **complexity** of the firm's structure must be examined.

Examiner's Tip

Computers form the backbone of most communication systems due to their efficient storing, handling and transmitting of information.

Scale and growth

Reasons for growth

- Larger size brings with it:
    - **improved survival prospects** through larger market share, diversification into different markets, and greater finance
    - **economies of scale**
    - an increased feeling of **status and power**.

Internal growth

- Also known as **organic** growth, this occurs when a firm expands, using its **own resources** by:
    - retaining its profits and liquid assets (cash)
    - using them to invest in additional fixed assets
    - thereby improving its productive capacity
    - and increasing its market share and growth.

Integration

- **External** growth, or integration, occurs when one firm takes over or merges with another.
- A **takeover** occurs when one firm obtains a controlling interest in another: it does not normally involve agreement between the firms.
- A **merger** takes place when two (or more) companies agree to combine their assets, and are reorganised as a result.
- **Horizontal integration** is found when firms producing **similar products or services** combine. The car industry provides many examples: e.g. Ford acquired Volvo, Volkswagen acquired Skoda.

	FORD	VOLVO
Founded	1903	1927
Founded by	Henry Ford	Assar Gabrielson Gustaf Larson
Turnover	£72.7 bn (1998)	£7.6 bn (1997)
Company value	£44 bn	£7.3 bn
Employees	364 000	28 000

	BP	AMOCO
Founded	1901	1889
Employees	56 000	43 000
Petrol stations	17 900	9300
Annual revenues	£44.4 bn	£22.5 bn
Barrels of oil pumped per day	3.3 million	1.2 million
Market worth	£46.3 bn	£24.1 bn

Figure 4.1 *The Ford/Volvo and BP/Amoco links*
Source: annual reports, 1999

(Continued next page)

STRUCTURE AND EFFICIENCY

Scale and growth

- The results of horizontal integration should be **larger-scale production** and **economies of scale**.
- The new company will have a greater market dominance since it now has the previous market share of the former companies.
- Companies in the same industry may decide to establish links as **joint ventures** rather than join formally. Such joint ventures avoid the expense and permanent commitment of a formal merger.

Vertical integration

- occurs when two firms in the same industry but at **different stages of production**, amalgamate.
- In '**vertical forwards**' integration, a firm amalgamates with one of its outlets: e.g. an oil company acquires a chain of petrol stations.
- '**Vertical backwards**' integration is when a firm moves back down the production chain to obtain one of its suppliers (e.g. food processing firm taking over an agricultural producer).
- Motives for vertical integration include:
  - **protection** – by the firm controlling outlets or suppliers
  - **control** – by the firm over quality, delivery and levels of supply, and of its market
  - **profits** – of the supplier/outlet now belong to the firm.

Lateral integration

- Also known as **conglomerate** or **diversified** integration, this occurs when firms in different industries and markets amalgamate.
- There may be some link between the firms' products, or the conglomerate may own quite different companies.
- The main advantage of lateral integration is **diversification**, i.e. not over-relying on a single product or market by **spreading risk**.
- Also, companies that were in a **saturated market** are no longer limited by that market.

Deintegration

- A company might reduce the scope of its activities. The main reason is **financial**: raising finance through selling a subsidiary, or cutting costs through the drive for efficiency.
- Deintegration occurs through **divestment** (selling a subsidiary that no longer fits into the company's long-term strategy) or **demerger**, where an existing company is split into two or more new divisions.
- Reasons for demerging include not achieving expected economies of scale, and the need to cut costs in times of economic downturn.

The resources to accomplish this transformation have been generated through selling our long-established metals business. Divestments have provided resources for subsequent acquisitions ... after the sale of its metals distribution business in May, the Group was able to acquire the leading German pipe systems company ... We then reverted to divestment ... and we shall now return to the acquisition process.

Source: Glynwed plc annual report and accounts, 1998 (extract)

Examiner's Tip

Arguments against integration include reduced competitiveness (diseconomies of scale), and over-borrowing due to increased costs.

Economies of scale

Internal economies of scale

- These are created when a firm's **unit cost of production falls as output increases**.
- The increased volume of production does not increase fixed costs: these costs are spread over a larger output, and as a result the average cost per unit falls.
- These economies are **measurable financially**: they can normally be quantified.

Types of internal economies

- Economies of **increased dimensions** arise from an increase in size: e.g. supertankers can carry many times the cargo volume compared with traditional tankers, which will more than offset the increase in running costs.
- **Financial economies**: larger firms find it easier to obtain loan capital, negotiating lower interest rates on these loans. Larger companies (PLCs) also have more, usually less expensive, sources of finance available.
- **Managerial economies**: growth in size leads to employment of specialist managers with greater levels of expertise. This is repeated in the benefits to larger firms from specialisation as a result of the division of labour.
- **Marketing economies**: larger firms can afford to pay for the services of specialist marketing companies, such as advertising agencies. A wider range of promotion becomes possible: the extra cost is spread over greater sales volume, which reduces the unit cost of promotion.
- **Purchasing economies**: larger firms can take advantage of bulk-buying discounts, which will reduce their unit material costs. They can also normally negotiate more favourable credit terms with their suppliers.
- **Risk-bearing economies**: firms grow larger through increasing their product range, this diversification allowing risk to be spread across more products and markets.
- **Technical economies**: the use of efficient, sophisticated technological equipment can often only be met by larger firms, who can also afford research and development costs which may lead to improved products and/or savings from technological breakthroughs.

External economies of scale

- These arise from a **growth in the size of the industry**, and all firms in the industry benefit from these economies.
- External economies have often been found where the industry is/was concentrated in a particular area.
- Examples include making china in the Potteries, shipbuilding in the north-east, and financial services in London.

Examples of external economies

- **Support.** Local firms provide specialist services, such as car component manufacturers in the Midlands supplying the local car industry.

- **Training.** Employees improve skills via local training providers supplying industry-specific courses. This pool of skilled labour is available to all firms in the area.

- **Information.** Local trade associations and chambers of commerce develop and provide specialist information.

- **Reputation.** Firms will benefit from an area's good name or reputation, e.g. 'Sheffield steel'.

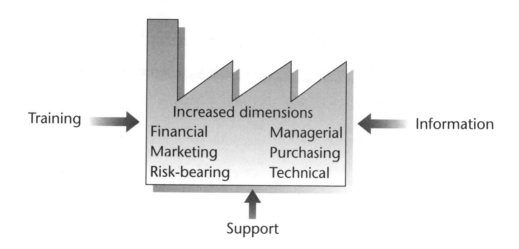

Figure 4.2 Internal and external economies of scale

Diseconomies of scale

- There are practical limits to the growth that can take place. Beyond a certain point, an organisation finds that its **unit costs start to increase**: it is now incurring diseconomies of scale.

- These diseconomies are not as quantitative as economies of scale, being **more qualitative** in nature. They arise for several reasons.

- The larger the firm, the more levels of hierarchy there tend to be for communication to flow through, leading to **greater bureaucracy**.

- This results in:

  - **worker dissatisfaction** and **poor labour relations**, which in turn may cause low morale and higher absenteeism

  - the **chain of command lengthening**, with decisions becoming slower to implement, reducing efficiency and therefore raising costs, and meaning that the firm is slower to react to changing (e.g. market) conditions.

STRUCTURE AND EFFICIENCY

Progress check

1 Identify TWO ways in which a company may use an organisation chart.

2 Distinguish between role and task cultures.

3 Distinguish between 'span of control' and 'chain of command'.

4 What are the benefits to managers and subordinates from successful delegation?

5 Give TWO examples of (a) formal, and (b) informal communication.

6 Why does the growth in a firm's size often cause communications to deteriorate?

7 What is the difference between horizontal and vertical integration?

8 What is the difference between internal and external economies of scale?

9 Why must managers be aware of diseconomies of scale?

Answers on page 90

Accounting and finance

The nature and purpose of accounting

The roles of the accounting function

- To make sound financial judgements, managers require information, provided by management accounting and financial accounting.
- Financial accounting involves:
  - collecting and recording information
  - analysing this information
  - presenting it to management
  - evaluating different sources of finance.
- Management accounting involves:
  - setting and controlling budgets
  - forecasting and controlling cashflow
  - classifying and calculating costs
  - making investment decisions.

Users of financial information

- These users may be internal or external to the firm.

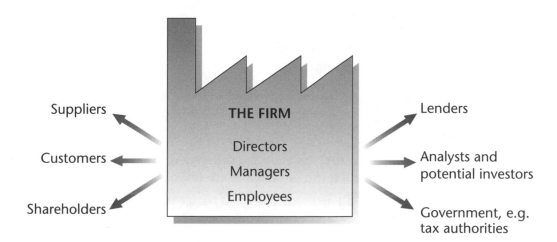

Figure 5.1 *Users of accounting information*

Examiner's Tip

Financial information deals with external influences on the firm: management accounting analyses the firm's internal operations.

Sources of finance

Internal sources

- Private sector firms can preserve cash through **retaining profits**, e.g. where a limited company decides to move profit to reserves rather than to distribute it as cash (share dividends).
- This is the main internal source of funds for many firms, although the source depends on the level of profits.

Control of working capital and cashflow

- The firm's cashflow and working capital can be improved by extending the average credit it takes from suppliers, and/or reducing the average credit period it allows its customers.
- Other controls include reducing stock levels and postponing the payment of expense creditors (e.g. electricity bill).

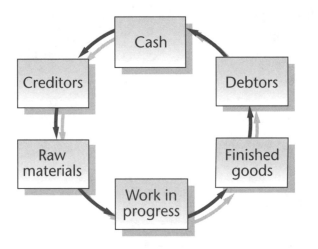

This shows the link between cash movements and working capital by providing a clear indication of the firm`s production cycle and credit periods allowed/taken.

Figure 5.2 The operating cycle

Sale of assets

- A firm may have surplus assets, e.g. during an economic recession or internal rationalisation, which can be sold to raise finance.
- The firm may sell an asset, then lease it back over time (**sale and leaseback**): the firm receives money, and can still use the asset.

External sources

- Associated with sole traders and partnerships, **family and friends** may provide low-cost finance needing little if any security.
- A limited company normally obtains most of its permanent capital by issuing ordinary and/or preference **shares**:
  - **ordinary (equity)** shareholders receive a variable dividend, which relies on surplus profits after all other payments: they may receive high dividends in times of high profits, and no dividend when profits are low;
  - **preference shares** have a fixed dividend and do not carry a vote, so – unlike ordinary shares – their issue does not affect the control of a company.

Group		1998		1997	
		Shares	$ million	Shares	$ million
Non-equity	8% (now 5.6% + tax credit) cumulative first preference shares of £1 each	7 232 838	12	7 232 838	12
	9% (now 6.3% + tax credit) cumulative second preference shares of £1 each	5 473 414	9	5 473 414	9
Equity	Ordinary shares of 50 pence each	9 683 010 023	4842	3 835 209 036	1918
	Ordinary shares of 25 pence each	–	–	5 762 583 600	2391
			4863		4330

Figure 5.3 Share capital, BP Amoco plc, 1998

Other long-term finance (normally five years and over)

- Using **long-term loans** for finance has certain advantages:
  - interest payments may be eroded by inflation
  - these payments are from gross profit (untaxed income), whereas dividend payments come out of (taxed) net profit
  - the lender has no direct say in the running of the firm.
- Unlike dividends, however, the interest payments must always be met, and failure to do so may lead to closure of the firm.
- **Debentures** and **mortgages** are popular forms of long-term loan.

Medium-term finance (between one and five years)

- **Bank loans** are fixed sums agreed between borrower and lender, for a fixed term. A special account is opened, interest being charged on the full balance, and security being required by the lender.
- With **leasing**, the firm obtains equipment without having to buy (own) it with a large capital outlay.
- Payments are known in advance, and can be made from cash generated by using the asset; over time, the asset can be upgraded, but the lessee (hirer) continues to pay for an item that is never owned.
- **Hire purchase** and **credit sale** agreements allow the buyer to acquire the asset immediately, and pay for it over time: however, the amount paid on credit far exceeds the original purchase price.

Short-term sources of finance (less than one year)

- **Overdrafts**, agreed with the bank, let a firm overdraw its account up to an agreed maximum for a charge on the amount overdrawn.
- Although usually less expensive and more flexible than loans, an overdraft facility can easily be withdrawn by the lender.
- **Factoring** is when a firm sells trade debts below face value to a factoring agent in return for immediate cash. The firm loses some of the debt's value, offset by quick receipt of cash which can be used immediately. The debt factor also takes on any bad debts.

Examiner's Tip

A firm's finance is normally determined by its **ownership** and **size**.

Financial accounting

Types of accounts

- Asset accounts record details of the **items owned** by a firm:
  - fixed assets are long-lasting, e.g. machinery, which depreciate and which are used indirectly to make profit
  - current assets – e.g. stocks, debtors and cash – fluctuate regularly and are used directly to make profit.
- **Liability** accounts record details of **amounts owing** by a firm:
  - the **capital** account shows the investment by the owner(s)
  - long-term liabilities are debts such as debentures not due to be repaid for at least one financial year
  - reserves (e.g. undistributed profits) are also long-term liabilities of limited companies
  - current liabilities are repayable within one year, and fluctuate regularly in value (e.g. overdraft, creditors).
- **Expense** accounts record the costs of the firm: e.g. rent, salaries, advertising, insurance, and cost of stationery.
- **Income** (revenue) accounts, e.g. sales, record trading results.

Final accounts

- Firms making the goods they sell will construct **manufacturing** accounts, to record costs of manufacture. These are either **prime costs** (direct production costs) or **factory overheads.**

The trading account

- Its purpose is to calculate **gross profit**, by deducting the firm's cost of sales from its sales income.

N. Merchant Trading account for year ending 31 December	£ (000)	£ (000)
Sales		400
Less cost of sales:		
Opening stock	55	
Purchases	290	
	345	
Less closing stock	(45)	
Gross profit	300	
		100

Figure 5.4 Trading account

The profit and loss account

- Its purpose is to calculate **net profit**, i.e. revenues less costs.

N. Merchant Profit and loss account for year ending 31 December	£ (000)	£ (000)
Gross profit		100
Less expenses:		
Administration	32	
Selling and distribution	16	
Financial	12	
		60
Net profit		**40**

Figure 5.5 Profit and loss account

The balance sheet

- Its purpose is to show the firm's **financial position** at a particular point in time.

N. Merchant Balance sheet as at 31 December	£ (000) Cost	£ (000) Depreciation	£ (000) Net
Fixed assets			
Land and buildings	100	–	100
Plant and equipment	24	6	18
Vehicles	5	3	2
	129	9	120
Current assets			
Stocks		45	
Debtors		25	
Bank and cash		20	
		90	
Current liabilities			
Creditors	20		
Accrued expenses	10		
Net current assets		30	
Net assets			60
			180
Capital			
Opening balance			140
Net profit for year			40
			180

Figure 5.6 Balance sheet

Examiner's Tip

Assets and liabilities appear in the firm's **balance sheet**: income and expenses are in the firm's **trading and profit and loss account**.

ACCOUNTING AND FINANCE

Using accounting information

- The firm's final accounts are interpreted by calculating ratios.
- Its present performance can then be compared with its performance in previous years, and with that of its competitors.

Interested groups

- The main interested groups are **managers**, **employees**, **lenders**, **investors** and the **government**. The key areas of interest are the firm's **profitability**, **liquidity** and **efficiency**.

Profitability ratios

- These compare a firm's profit with the resources used to make it.
- **Return on capital employed** (ROCE) shows the profitability of the investment by calculating its percentage return.
- This return can be compared with other investment returns, to indicate whether it is worth the owner(s) staying in business.
- **Net profit margin** (NP ratio, or NP %) shows the percentage of turnover – sales – represented by net profit, i.e. how many pence out of every £1 sold is net profit.
- The NP margin will fall if the gross profit margin has also fallen, or if the firm's other expenses as a percentage of sales have risen.
- **Gross profit margin** (GP ratio, or GP %) indicates the percentage of turnover represented by gross profit.

Liquidity ratios

- These ratios show if the firm is **overtrading**: expanding without enough long-term capital, putting pressure on its working capital.
- The **working capital** (current) ratio discloses the firm's liquidity position. If current liabilities exceed current assets, the firm may have difficulty in meeting its debts.
- **Liquid ratio** ('acid test' or 'quick assets') shows if the firm can meet short-term debts without having to sell any stock.
- **Debtors' collection period** ('Debtor days') measures how efficient the firm is at collecting its debts.
- Creditors' collection period ('Creditor days') calculates the average length of credit the firm receives from its suppliers.

Asset efficiency ratios

- **Rate of stock turnover** ('Stockturn') calculates how often the firm sells its stock, indicating how efficient stock management is.
- **Capital gearing** analyses the different types of payments made to capital: **variable-rate return** (ordinary share dividends) compared with **fixed-rate return** (preference dividends and loan interest). Gearing is important when additional capital is required.

Capital and revenue expenditure in final accounts

- Asset and expense accounts record purchases made by a business.

- These purchases are analysed under two headings:

Capital expenditure	Revenue expenditure
the firm buys new (or improves existing) fixed assets (e.g. buys a new delivery van) shown in the balance sheet	the firm pays its everyday running expenses (e.g. pays rent, pays wages) shown in the profit and loss account

- Capital expenditure does not affect profit calculation, but revenue expenditure does. If expenditure is classified incorrectly, the profit figure will also be incorrect.

Investment decisions

- Payback calculates the time taken for an investment to recoup its initial outlay.

- Thus an investment of £120 000 that generates net cash flows of £12 000 a month has a 10-month payback period.

- Although easy to calculate, the payback method does not show how **profitable** the investment is.

- The **accounting rate of return** (ARR) method compares profit with cash invested:

$$\frac{\text{average annual return}}{\text{investment outlay}} \times 100$$

- Although this method shows the investments' profitability, it **ignores the timing** of the cash flows.

Examiner's Tip

Liquidity measures the firm's ability to survive in the short run. Profitability indicates its ability to survive in the longer term.

Budgeting and forecasting

Budgeting

- A **budget** is a plan expressed in money, which relates to a given time period.
- Budgets allow a firm's activities to be **co-ordinated** through a master budget, **controlled** through comparing actual with budgeted performance, and **communicated** by involving all staff.
- Budgeting is subject to the **principal budget factor**: the item that limits the firm's activities. The most common principal budget factor is demand for the products: other examples include the availability of materials or skilled labour, and machine capacity.

The main budgets

- Budgets can be prepared for each major function of the firm.

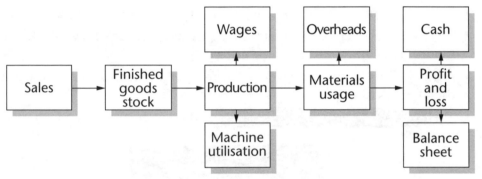

Figure 5.7 *The main budgets*

- A **budgeted profit and loss** account and **balance sheet** will be prepared from a range of the functional budgets shown above.
- The cash budget summarises expected cash inflows and outflows.

Budgetary control

- Managers compare the expected (budgeted) performance of their department with its actual performance.
- Control is through **management by exception**: any difference between budgeted and actual performance produces a **variance**, which may be:
  - **favourable** – e.g. where actual sales exceed budgeted, or where a particular cost comes in below budget; or
  - **adverse** (unfavourable) – e.g. actual sales have not reached target, or an actual cost is above its budgeted level.
- For example, here is a cost and income summary for a firm:

	Budget (£)	Actual (£)
Sales income	250 000	260 000
Labour costs	80 000	85 000
Materials costs	40 000	38 000
Overheads	10 000	11 000
Profit (sales less costs)	120 000	126 000

- Actual profit is £6000 higher than budgeted profit.
- The variances making up this difference are:
  - sales – £10 000 favourable (actual revenue is higher than budgeted)
  - labour – £5000 adverse (actual cost is higher than budget)
  - material – £2000 favourable (actual cost is lower)
  - overheads – £1000 adverse (actual cost is higher).
- Overall, the £12 000 total favourable variances less the £6000 total adverse ones give this £6000 overall favourable position.
- Some variances are due to factors **controllable** by individual managers, who can only be accountable for controllable variances: e.g. the manager may have authorised a lower selling price in the hope that, by selling more, the product's **price elasticity** will lead to increased total revenue.
- Other variances may not be under the manager's control, e.g. an adverse wages variance due to an unexpected national pay rise.

Cash flow forecasting

- Cash flow is sometimes confused with profit: the assumption is that, if a firm makes £1 million profit after tax, it has also increased its cash and bank balance by £1 million.
- Large profits can be made, and yet the cash and bank balances may at the same time have fallen. Reasons include:
  - cash is used to buy fixed assets (this has no great effect on the profit figure)
  - sales are made on credit (no immediate cash, but profit increases)
  - suppliers are paid quickly (cash falls, with no effect on profit).
- **Credit control** is an important function for any business trying to control its cashflow.
- Cash flow forecasts are therefore used: any forecast will be inaccurate, e.g. actual sales will differ from forecast sales.
- The firm's directors will therefore need to **monitor** the **accuracy** of the cash-flow forecast, and take appropriate action.
- If the forecast indicates that cash-flow must be improved, the directors have a number of options. They can:
  - calculate 'debtor days' and 'creditor days' ratios to assess credit periods taken and allowed
  - factor their debts
  - consider sale and leaseback
  - examine other ways of controlling working capital, e.g. by reducing stock levels.

Examiner's Tip

It is almost as important to identify large cash surpluses as it is large cash deficits, to ensure surplus cash is used efficiently.

Cost classification and analysis

Classifying costs

- Classifying costs allows **analysis** to take place: e.g. break-even analysis requires costs to be split into **fixed** and **variable**.

- Classifying costs as **direct** or **indirect** is necessary for **absorption costing**, a costing method that 'absorbs' overheads into product costs: e.g. factory rent (a factory overhead) must be absorbed into the cost of products made in the factory.

Direct and indirect costs

- Direct costs are linked with **particular product lines**: they are costs that can be identified precisely with a product or process.

- Indirect costs (**overheads**) are shared between product lines, because they **do not relate to one product** in particular. In practice, these costs are apportioned to the different products.

- For example, a car manufacturer has sheet steel and engine parts as direct materials, assembly-line employees as direct labour, and the cost of transporting product-specific items (e.g. engine parts) as direct expenses. Indirect costs include supervisory wages and business rates.

Fixed and variable costs

- This classification is based on the way that **costs behave when output changes**.

- Fixed costs remain **constant** as output changes. Factory rent and business rates are two examples often given, although in practice rent is a **stepped** cost: as output increases, the firm needs extra space, and at some stage will have to pay additional rent.

- Variable costs **change** in proportion to changes in output: e.g. doubling output typically doubles the cost of materials required.

- **Semi-variable** costs are found in practice: e.g. power costs often include a fixed element (a standing charge) and a variable element based on the amount of power used.

Break-even analysis

- The break-even point can be calculated mathematically and/or displayed graphically.

- Every product made has a variable cost: it also has a (higher) selling price. The difference between these two figures is the **contribution** made by the product towards the firm's fixed costs.

- When enough of these individual contributions have been made, the firm's total costs are covered and it is at break-even point, making neither a profit nor a loss.

- **Contribution = selling price less variable cost.**

- Break-even point $= \dfrac{\text{fixed costs}}{\text{unit contribution}}$

- If a firm's fixed costs are £6000, variable costs are £1 per unit and its selling price is £2.50:
  - unit contribution is £2.50 less £1.00 = £1.50
  - break-even point is £6000/£1.50 = 4000 units
- The firm must make and sell 4000 units to break even: every unit sold above this increases net profit by £1.50, and every unit sold below 4000 produces a loss of £1.50. At an output of 4000 units, total revenue and total costs are both £10 000 (break-even point).
- If the firm makes and sells 6000 units, its **margin of safety** – the number of units by which production and sales can fall before it starts to make a loss – is 2000 units. Its profit will be:
  - total revenue = 6000 x £2.50   = £15 000
  - total costs (fixed 6000 + variable 6000)   = £12 000
  - profit   = £3 000

Graphical display

- The above data is used to construct the chart below.

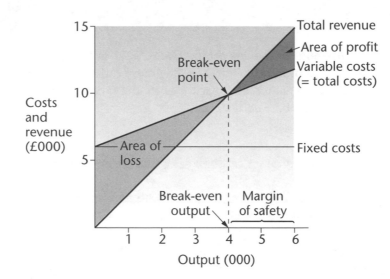

Figure 5.8 Break-even chart

Limitations of break-even analysis

- Not all costs can be easily classified as fixed or variable (e.g. those semi-variable costs with a standing charge).
- Sales prices are assumed constant at all activity levels.
- Production and sales are assumed to be the same figure.
- Fixed costs may change with output (e.g. stepped costs).
- Unit variable costs may also change, due to economies of scale.

Examiner's Tip

Break-even analysis is helpful to management when planning the firm's production and sales.

Progress check

1 What is the purpose of (a) a profit and loss account; (b) a balance sheet?

2 State the difference between leasing and credit sale.

3 Give THREE differences between shares and debentures.

4 What is the difference between budgeting and budgetary control?

5 How does cash-flow forecasting aid the survival of a firm?

6 Balance sheet extracts (end of 2001): cash £60 000; debtors £150 000; creditors £160 000; tax owing £300 000. The debtors will pay in January; the creditors will be paid January (50%) and February (50%); tax will be paid in March.

Year 2002 forecast:	Jan	Feb	Mar	Apr	May	Jun
Sales £ (000)	120	600	600	400	120	120
Materials £ (000)	80	80	90	90	90	90

Other information for the first 6 months of 2002: Sales are on one month's credit, materials on two months' credit. Monthly overheads are £45 000, payable in the same month. Wages are paid in cash each month: the monthly wage bill is £90 000. New shares will be issued in February: £50 000.

Prepare a cash budget.

7 Distinguish between direct and indirect costs, giving an example of each.

8 Calculate the break-even point for a firm with fixed costs of £110 000, unit variable costs of £3.45 and a selling price of £8.95.

Answers on page 91

People in organisations

Human resource planning

HRM functions

Area	Reasons: to
Workforce planning	identify and meet labour shortfalls; review employees' current skills.
Recruitment and selection	ensure objectives are met; bring in new ideas; appoint qualified and skilled employees.
Training and development	help new employees settle in quickly; help them develop and contribute more to the organisation.
Appraisal	encourage employees to achieve their potential; support employees in achieving personal goals.
Welfare	help employees satisfy their personal needs.
Consultation and negotiation	communicate key policies; motivate employees through involvement; anticipate and identify employee concerns.

Workforce planning

- Workforce planning seeks to ensure that workforce **requirements** are identified, **levels** guarantee that production takes place, **quality** leads to improved productivity, and **costs** meet set targets.

- Workforce plans are often based on a **STEP** analysis of the external influences on the organisation:

  - **Social** – e.g. increased numbers of women returning to work

  - **Technological** – e.g. new processes requiring new skills

  - **Economic** – e.g. free movement of labour in the EU

  - **Political** – e.g. government training schemes.

- A firm's workforce strategy is influenced by **supply and demand**.

If the labour supply exceeds the firm's demand for labour:	If the firm's demand for labour exceeds its supply:
• voluntary or compulsory redundancy	• additional advertising
• redeployment and retraining	• retraining programmes
• encouraging early retirement	• better labour market competitiveness (pay rates)
• encouraging 'natural wastage'	

Examiner's Tip

The key function of HRM is to ensure the right number of employees, of the right quality, in the right place, at the right time.

Recruitment, selection and training

Labour turnover (LTO)

- LTO benefits a firm by introducing new staff with new ideas, although high LTO may indicate:
  - low morale amongst the employees
  - pay levels that are below comparable local rates
  - high costs of recruitment and training.

Recruitment and selection

- The choice of recruitment and selection procedures depends on the **post** under consideration, **cost**, **coverage** and the **time** available.
- Job descriptions and person specifications are prepared when recruiting staff:
  - the **job description** contains details of the post (title and location), tasks and employment conditions
  - the **person specification** outlines experience, qualifications and special aptitudes required by the appointee.
- **External recruitment** sources include advertising (local papers, national press, specialist publications), Job Centres, careers offices and employment agencies.
- Semi-skilled workers are likely to be recruited using local papers and Job Centres, whereas senior executives are more likely to be recruited nationally (or internationally) through 'headhunting' and national press advertising.
- An alternative is to recruit **internally**, e.g. by promotion. The employee is known to the firm and is familiar with work routines; staff morale and motivation improves, and it is less expensive.
- However, internal recruitment limits the firm's choice and will not bring new ideas in from outside.

Selection

- **Interviews** are the most popular selection method. They may be formal or informal, and conducted on a one-to-one or group basis.
- The interview has the advantage of being a two-way process but is not **reliable** as a form of selection, often being subjective.

- The **interviewer** can assess
  - oral communication skills
  - physical appearance
  - personal attributes.

- The **interviewee** can assess
  - physical working conditions
  - future prospects
  - the working atmosphere.

- Other selection procedures include:
  - **aptitude tests** and simulations used to test the candidate's skills and ability to carry out the duties of the post
  - **achievement testing**, to see if the candidate still has the relevant skills
  - **personality tests** to measure the candidate's personality 'type'
  - **intelligence tests** to check the candidate's reasoning and mental abilities.

Training and development

- **Induction training** introduces a new employee to the firm, and the firm to the new employee. It makes the employee comfortable – and therefore motivated and productive – as quickly as possible.

- **Internal** (on-the-job) training is where employees learn as they work. Training is usually limited to particular skills or procedures and uses work manuals.

- Internal training is easy to organise, it can be adapted to the trainee's needs, and is relatively inexpensive and job-specific.

- It can, however, disrupt work; the trainer may not have training skills and/or may be a poor communicator; bad work practices will be continued and new methods are not introduced into the firm.

- **External** (off-the-job) training is where staff learn off-site (e.g. at a local college). Advantages to the firm are that:
  - specialist trainers are used
  - general theories and ideas are introduced
  - training can be intensive
  - training occurs away from job distractions.

- However, this training can be expensive, it is isolated from work and the trainee is away from the workplace and is not productive.

Appraisal

- By appraising staff, managers seek to improve **present performance** through identifying individual strengths and weaknesses, and **future performance** by identifying individuals for development.

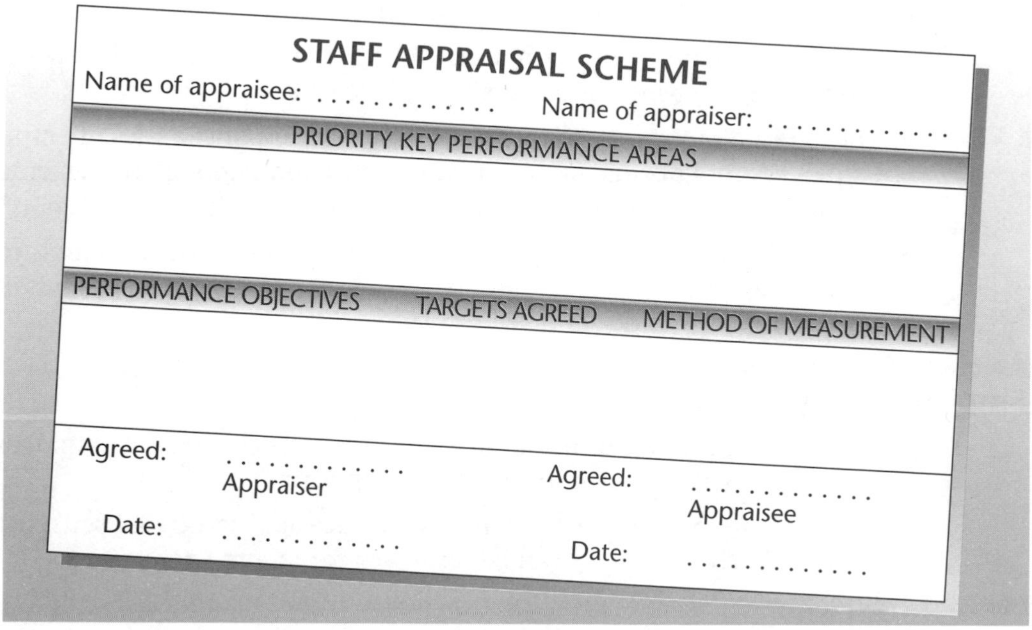

STAFF APPRAISAL SCHEME

Name of appraisee: . . . .   Name of appraiser: . . . .

PRIORITY KEY PERFORMANCE AREAS

PERFORMANCE OBJECTIVES	TARGETS AGREED	METHOD OF MEASUREMENT

Agreed: . . . .   Appraiser

Date: . . . .

Agreed: . . . .   Appraisee

Date: . . . .

Figure 6.1 Document from a company staff appraisal scheme

Examiner's Tip

Costs of not training include demotivated staff, low productivity, increased absenteeism, dissatisfied customers and loss of sales.

Legislation and work

Employee protection

- Under The **Health and Safety at Work Act** (HASAWA) 1974, employers must take **all reasonable care** to ensure the safety of employees.
- They must provide appropriate training and instruction on health and safety matters, and are obliged to provide safe:
  - working environments
  - plant and systems of work
  - entry and exit arrangements
  - working processes (e.g. for unsafe materials).
- The **obligations of employees** under HASAWA are to:
  - co-operate with the employer on health and safety matters
  - take reasonable care of themselves and others at work
  - not interfere with anything provided for their safety
  - report defects in workplace equipment and processes.
- **Enforcement** of HASAWA is by the Health and Safety Executive (HSE), which carries out investigations by its inspectors, develops new health and safety laws and standards and publishes guidance.
- The **Control of Substances Hazardous to Health** (COSHH) regulations are based on HASAWA provisions and require employers to control, monitor and carry out relevant training.

European Union health and safety protection

- EU member states have harmonised health and safety provisions within a legal framework, to ensure employers use safe practices.
- The **Safety Framework Directive** outlines the responsibilities of employers and employees for encouraging workplace health and safety improvements. Specific requirements include manual handling of heavy loads and machinery safety.
- The **Working Time Regulations** set minimum standards for employees (with some exceptions) for a maximum weekly working time: these Regulations also set minimum **rest periods** and **annual leave**.

Employment protection

- Employers must give **written particulars** of their contract of employment to employees within three months of starting work.
- Workers employed under a contract of service are protected against **unfair dismissal**. The employee can be dismissed for incompetence, gross or serious misconduct (e.g. assault, dishonesty), or through the post becoming redundant.
- **Remedies** for unfair dismissal include reinstatement, re-engagement in a comparable job or compensation.
- Recent EU measures being implemented in the UK include:
  - **Parental Leave Directive** – the right of employees to three months' unpaid leave after the birth or adoption of a child
  - **Part-time Work Directive** – providing for the equal treatment of part-time workers with full-time employees.

Discrimination

- The **Sex Discrimination Acts** (1975 and 1986) make it unlawful for employers to discriminate on the grounds of sex when they advertise a job, recruit staff and set retirement dates.
- The **Race Relations Acts** (1968 and 1976) make it unlawful to discriminate on race, colour, nationality and ethnic origin.
- Figure 6.2 shows, for each age group, lower unemployment rates for white people than for people from the other ethnic groups.

(Great Britain)	Percentages				
	16–24	25–34	35–44	45 and over	All ages
White	13	6	5	5	6
Black	39	18	12	16	19
Indian	18	7	6	7	8
Pakistani/Bangladeshi	29	16	13	26	21
Other groups	22	13	10	8	13
All ethnic groups	**14**	**7**	**5**	**5**	**7**

Figure 6.2 *Unemployment by ethnic group and age, 1997–8*
Source: ONS, 1999

- The **Disability Discrimination Act** (1995) makes it unlawful for disabled persons to be treated less favourably than others.
- The **Equal Pay Act** (1970) requires equal rates of pay for men and women doing the same job, or work of 'equivalent value'. This principle was reinforced by the EU in its Directive on equal pay.

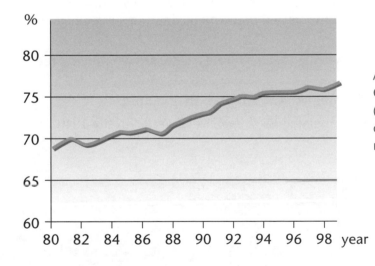

According to the Equal Opportunities Commission (1999), the UK ranks tenth out of the 15 EU countries regarding equality of pay.

Figure 6.3 *Women's pay as percentage of men's pay*
Source: ONS, 1999

Examiner's Tip

Issues of discrimination in business relate to an organisation's social responsibility and ethical stance.

Motivation

Motivation theory

- Theorists differ on what makes a job 'satisfying', such as:
  - pay levels
  - work environment
  - nature of work tasks
  - degree of job security
  - organisational culture
  - working hours
  - fringe benefits
  - management styles
  - promotion prospects

Classical theory

- These theorists studied organisational behaviour by examining the **nature of the work** being done.

- **F W Taylor** used scientific management principles to separate jobs into their elements: this aspect of his work led to the development of **work study** and **method study** principles. Taylor believed that high pay acted as the prime motivator, largely ignoring morale and other influences.

- The work of the classical theorists is regarded as being limited and has been modified by later theorists.

Human relations and content theories

- These theorists concentrate on **people's needs**, and not exclusively on the job being done, defining the organisation in terms of its **social environment**.

- **Elton Mayo** researched into groups at the Hawthorne works of the Western Electric Company (1927 to 1932). He kept changing working conditions, discovering that output increased even when conditions worsened. His conclusions were:

  - that the employees being observed were a close group enjoying the attention given to them

  - this increased their self-esteem, and thus their output.

- **Abraham Maslow** formulated his 'hierarchy of needs' in the 1940s.

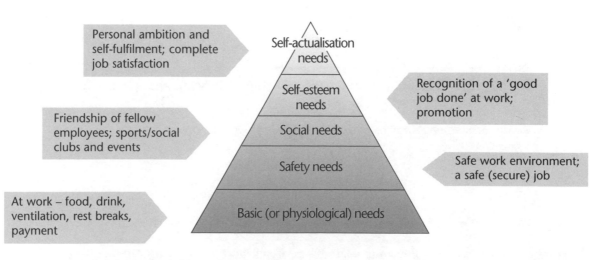

Figure 6.4 Maslow's hierarchy of needs

- At any time, one group of needs is dominant, and these must be met before the employee proceeds to the next group. In a work context, employees must have the opportunity to **fulfil** these needs.
- **Frederick Herzberg** analysed needs as **motivators**, which relate to work content and to Maslow's higher-order needs, and **hygiene factors**, which relate to the working environment and Maslow's lower-order needs.
- While hygiene factors should be present (motivation falls if they are neglected), they do not by themselves motivate employees.

Motivators	**Hygiene factors**
• achievement	• company policies
• recognition	• status
• responsibility	• supervision
• promotion	• security
• the work itself	• working conditions
	• money

- **Douglas McGregor** analysed two opposing attitudes concerning the formal organisation of workers.
- **Theory X** management – his negative attitude – assumes people dislike and will avoid work, and must be controlled and directed towards achieving organisational objectives.
- **Theory Y** management assumes employees can exercise their own control, and can learn to seek and accept responsibility.
- Theory X links with the work of earlier classical theorists, and suggests money is the main motivator; Theory Y recognises the importance of Maslow's higher-order needs in motivating employees.
- Theory X suggests an authoritarian form of organisational structure; Theory Y argues that the main limiting factors in a firm are management's ability to channel employee potential.
- Specific problems arise when employees expecting Theory Y management are subject to Theory X, or vice versa.
- The Japanese approaches to management have been called 'Theory Z', which recognises the Japanese emphasis on human relations at work and on employment for life.

Process theories

- These theories analyse the thinking, or expectations, behind decisions made by employees.
- **V H Vroom's Expectancy Theory** argues that motivation depends on two factors: how attractive the outcome is, and the degree of expectation that the action will produce this hoped-for outcome.
- This theory suggests managers must analyse employees' motives, and ensure they have realistic goals to achieve.

Examiner's Tip

Maslow's ideas illustrate the importance of work to individuals, and help explain some of the social costs of high unemployment.

Motivation in practice

Management and leadership styles

- A **democratic** manager (associated with Theory Y) guides and advises, but involves the group in decision-making.
- An **autocratic** manager (linked to Theory X) might allow group involvement, but decision-making stays at the top.
- A **laissez-faire** manager chooses not to interfere in the work of the group: this approach can be successful if there are **cohesive groups** prepared to work in achieving common objectives.
- The 'best' management/leadership style is determined by:
  - management training
  - awareness of different styles
  - individual manager's preferences
  - organisational culture
  - organisational size and complexity
  - stage of the firm's evolution.

Overcoming poor motivation

- Poor motivation causes employee dissatisfaction and alienation, leading to high labour turnover, increased absenteeism and sickness, poor timekeeping, and more disputes in the firm.
- Firms try to avoid these occurring through strategies:
  - **changing leadership styles** – e.g. a more democratic style
  - establishing **teamwork** – to develop a 'common purpose'
  - reviewing **pay levels** – e.g. offering incentives
  - ensuring **greater staff involvement** – e.g. quality circles
  - **job enrichment** – allowing staff to use their full abilities.
- To increase involvement and motivation, firms with over 1000 employees in EU states (and at least 150 in each of two member states) must set up a works council or other procedure to inform and consult staff on key issues.
- This EU Directive illustrates the drive nowadays to promote partnership between employers and employees.

Remuneration

- Payment systems may be **incentive-based** (e.g. a piece rate per item produced) or **time-based**, such as an annual salary, or may **combine** the two (e.g. overtime at an increased hourly rate).
- **Fringe benefits** also exist: e.g. a company car, subsidised meals and travel, and private health schemes.
- **Profit-sharing** and **share ownership** schemes motivate employees by making them (feel) part of the firm's success. Such schemes now exist in about three-quarters of all UK public companies.

Examiner's Tip

When an employee is given a task to carry out, and it is carried out badly, this may be due to poor motivation and not a lack of ability.

Progress check

1 Why is workforce planning undertaken by a firm?

2 How will an organisation use STEP analysis to assess its labour force strategy?

3 How does the Personnel department help a firm achieve labour targets?

4 How do organisations benefit from operating safe practices?

5 What forms of discrimination still exist at work, and what legislation exists to counter them?

6 How should analysis of Herzberg influence the work of firms?

7 In what practical ways can a firm improve motivation?

Answers on page 92

Marketing

The marketing function

Marketing function and objectives

- The marketing function has three key roles in a business. It
  - supports the exchange process through **techniques aimed at the consumer**
  - **collects and analyses data** on the consumer and the market
  - acts as a **co-ordinating** function for the organisation.
- The traditional production-led approach focuses on the product.
- A **market-led firm** examines its activities through the eyes of its customers.
- This type of firm sets clear marketing objectives and reviews its other objectives in the light of these: e.g. an objective to increase market share will affect other objectives based on production and cash-flow.

Figure 7.1 Marketing influence on the business cycle

Markets and segmentation

Markets

- **Consumer markets** exist for consumer goods, bought for their own satisfaction.
- **Single-use consumer goods** have short lives and are income-inelastic: often called FMCGs ('fast-moving consumer goods'), they satisfy physical (e.g. food), psychological (e.g. cosmetics) or impulse (e.g. sweets) needs.
- **Consumer durables** (e.g. DVD players, televisions) have an income-elastic demand: they are long-lasting, expensive, bought infrequently and with care.
- **Consumer services** (e.g. hairdressers, plumbers) are used more often as income grows, and tend to satisfy basic physical and safety needs.
- **Industrial markets** contain products used by industries in their production.
- Industrial goods are classified as **capital goods** (e.g. new equipment), industrial consumables (e.g. fuel, stationery) and **industrial services** (such as cleaning).

	Consumer markets	**Industrial markets**
Customers	Many: allowing price to be set by the firm	Few: firm negotiates price and terms with the customer
Channel	Various, e.g. through wholesalers and retailers	Usually direct to customer
Product	More standardised: some differentiation	More personalised: may be made to end-user requirements
Methods	Resources concentrated on advertising: mass media used	Less generalised: more personal selling, use of specialist journals

Market segmentation

- Segmenting a market involves dividing it into **distinct subgroups**, using either the product or the consumer as the basis for segmentation.
- Consumers are often segmented according to the following characteristics:
  - **age**: e.g. saving and spending habits change with age. Banks, holiday firms and clothing manufacturers are examples of businesses targeting different age-related segments;
  - **sex**: some products (e.g. cosmetics) are gender-influenced; others may be targeted at one sex (e.g. brewers targeting certain brands of drinks at men, and other brands at women);
  - **socio-economic** status: marketers use a scale to summarise occupational and social class groupings, identifying consumer groups by characteristics, e.g. income, education, leisure. This influences the targeting of advertising, e.g. tabloid (*The Mirror*) or broadsheet (*The Guardian*) newspapers;

(Continued next page)

Markets and segmentation

How we see ourselves
% who describe themselves as

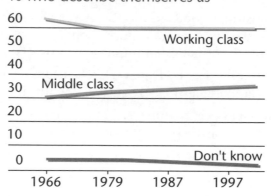

	1966	1979	1987	1997

Working class — Middle class — Don't know

Social grade
% of total population

1975

- 9.5 (E)
- A 2.3
- 10.4 (B)
- 23.5 (C1)
- 21.8 (D)
- 32.5 (C2)

1997–8

- 11.59 (E)
- A 2.86
- 17.99 (B)
- 18.11 (D)
- 27.53 (C1)
- 21.93 (C2)

A Upper middle class
Higher managerial, administrative or professional

B Middle class
Intermediate managerial, administrative or professional

C1 Lower middle class
Supervisory or clerical and junior managerial, administrative or professional

C2 Skilled working class
Skilled manual workers

D Working class
Semi- and unskilled manual workers

E Lowest subsistence level
State pensioners or widows (no other earner), casual or lowest grade workers

Figure 7.2 *Social grade*
Source: NRS and British Election Study, 1999

- **national**, **regional** and **local** factors: income, tastes and leisure vary between cultures, and from area to area;

- **psychographic profiling**: these profiles use lifestyles to segment consumers and products: e.g. differentiating a car by emphasising different features (safety, economy, styling, power, carrying capacity) to different 'lifestyle' customers (e.g. young single driver; family of four).

- Firms concentrating on small market segments are carrying out **niche marketing**: they create a known name and image, and establish a market position.

- Problems for niche marketers are:

  - the firm may have to **remain small** because overheads need to be kept low (if competitors benefit from economies of scale, they will be price-competitive)

  - there is **no diversification** – the single-product approach depends for its success on consumer demand levels and tastes remaining at least constant.

Examiner's Tip

The targeted market segments influence the nature of the product, price, place and promotion used.

Market research

Sources of information

- Firms use different methods to analyse their market performance.
- Information is needed about consumer habits and spending patterns, products, markets and the firm itself.

SWOT analysis

- This analyses a firm's (internal) **strengths** and **weaknesses**, and its (external) **opportunities** and **threats**.
- A company selling garden sheds, which plans to diversify into greenhouses, may find a SWOT analysis identifies these factors:
  - (S) – existing contacts/outlets; known trade name; good reputation; existing suppliers of glass and wood; motivated staff.
  - (W) – employees lack skills; no knowledge of the market for greenhouses; limited capital for expansion.
  - (O) – diversify to spread risk; reduce the seasonal effect of shed sales; no major local or regional competitor.
  - (T) – most competitors are large, so difficult to compete (fewer economies of scale) on price.

The Boston growth and market share matrix

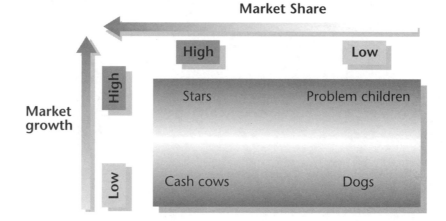

Figure 7.3 Boston Box analysis

- **'Stars'** are potentially highly profitable: large investment is needed to develop and promote them into 'cash cows'.
- **'Problem children'**: in a slow-growth segment, they plug a hole in the product range but if not disposed of they may become 'dogs'.
- **'Cash cows'**: the key to the firm's profits and sales; it keeps investing in them, and they help finance the development of 'stars' – but if not managed properly they risk becoming 'dogs'.
- **'Dogs'** are heavy users of resources, but remain unprofitable: the firm rids itself of these unless they can be made profitable.
- The Boston Box analysis is particularly suitable for larger companies which have a wide product range.

Researching the market

- The purpose of market research is to obtain information on market conditions for the firm's products. It concentrates on:
  - the **product**:
    - What stage is it at in its life-cycle?
    - Can it be improved or its life be extended?
    - Is its price competitive?
    - How effective is its promotion and distribution?
  - the **market**:
    - What is its total size and how is it segmented?
    - Is it expanding or contracting, or seasonal?
    - Is it easy for new firms to enter?
  - the **competition**:
    - Who are the main competitors?
    - What are their pricing and promotion policies?

The type of research

- **Field** (or **primary**) research collects original data, using various techniques.
  - **Questionnaires** are designed specifically for the task, and completed face-to-face, by telephone or through post/email.
  - **Test marketing**: a potential product is marketed regionally to gauge reaction to it, before committing the firm to production and national launch.
  - **Consumer panels**: consumers make comments on the product.
  - **Observation**: people's reactions (e.g. to a new display) are observed whilst they shop.
- If field research is to provide relevant information, it must use a **representative sample**: consumers forming the sample must represent the market as a whole.
- The sampling method used may be **random** (all in the population have an equal chance of selection) or **stratified** (a subgroup of the population is selected, e.g. using age or sex), or a **quota** may be set with data collected until the target quota is met.
- The firm must select the right people (the **sampling method**), and enough people (the **sample size**). The **cost** of collecting the data and the **time** taken to collect it, are key factors in the decision.
- **Desk** (or **secondary**) research uses existing information such as the firm's own sales figures, official publications (e.g. from Office of National Statistics), trade associations and chambers of commerce, market research agency reports and newspaper reports.
- Firms undertake **quantitative research** – factual information (e.g. units sold, market share) – or **qualitative research**, concentrating on attitudes and opinions (consumer tastes, likes and dislikes).

Examiner's Tip

Desk research is undertaken for other purposes so the data are not always relevant, although it is cheaper than field research and is normally quicker to obtain.

Marketing the product

The product mix

- A firm's product mix – the complete range of products in all markets and segments – consists of different product lines (the group of products aimed at one market segment).
- The **mix width** identifies the number of product lines: the wider the width, the more diversified the firm is and the better chance it has of surviving if a particular market segment collapses.
- **Mix depth** shows the number of different products in a single product line. The deeper the depth, the more segments the firm operates in, avoiding its products competing with each other.

The product life-cycle

- Firms develop new products to maintain product mix. A new product may be **innovative** (the original model/type, e.g. Sony Walkman), **imitative** (which copies the original), or **replacement** (new model).
- A product has only a limited life once introduced on the market. A firm therefore needs a balanced product portfolio (product mix), replacing those in maturity and decline with newer products.

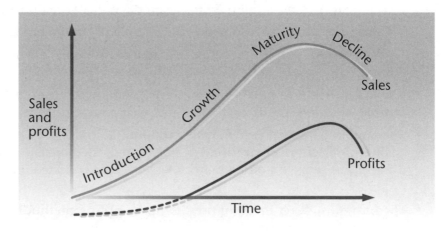

Figure 7.4 *Stages of the product life-cycle*

- **Introduction.** Following planning and development, the product is introduced onto the market. Characteristics of this stage are:
  - low sales, limited knowledge and no consumer loyalty
  - heavy promotion to build its image and consumer confidence
  - losses due to heavy development and promotion costs
  - limited distribution levels, but high stockholding for the manufacturer.
- Attempts are made to gain market share, e.g. through penetration pricing, but there remains a high chance of product failure.
- **Growth.** As consumer knowledge and loyalty grow, sales increase profits (helped by economies of scale) start. Competitors may introduce similar products, or adapt price and promotion policies.
- The product is changing from a 'star' into a 'cash cow'.

- **Maturity**. Growth slows with saturation sales. Profits are being maximised, but the firm has to defend its market position. Sales are maintained by promotion, customer loyalty and product differentiation through alterations such as new packaging.

- **Decline**. Total sales fall for the firm. To counter this, the firm may reduce prices, cutting into its profit margin. Production may be maintained if other firms abandon their products, in an attempt to gain a larger share of the (smaller) market.

Extending product life

- Extending product life extends the maturity (high-profits) stage.

- The firm may try extending an existing product's life by altering:

  - the product – renewing the image (a 'new improved' model); extending it into other formats (e.g. ice-cream Mars)

  - the marketing strategy – changing the image or appeal (e.g. personal computers being used for leisure as well as work).

- Product life-cycle analysis may overstate the importance of developing new products rather than seeking to extend the lives of existing ones. The four stages are not always easily separated, and the life-cycle can become a self-fulfilling prophecy.

Product differentiation and branding

- Product differentiation explores how consumers view products.

- The product may be different (e.g. better designed or made), or may be **perceived** as different, due to advertising or branding.

- Product differentiation is helped where a product has a **unique selling point** (USP), a feature which the firm can focus on to differentiate it from competitor products.

- **Branding** assures consumers that their next purchase will be identical to their last purchase. This creates **brand loyalty**.

- Through branding:

  - a respected brand name helps sell new products
  - brand loyalty leads to repeat purchases
  - retailers will give display space to the branded product
  - the brand name can be placed in another market
  - market segmentation becomes easier.

- **Own-label** brands carry the retailer's name. The retailer buys from a manufacturer after agreeing quality standards rather than from a major brand supplier, and sells the own-brand goods at competitive prices. The manufacturer benefits from using excess capacity.

- Branding relies on **packaging**, which carries the brand name, gives product information that must be legally displayed, and offers space used to persuade the consumer to buy the product.

- Modern packaging offers a communication base, ease of display, impact and environmental acceptability.

Examiner's Tip

Product life-cycle analysis determines other marketing policy, e.g. how the product is advertised, distributed, priced and developed.

Pricing decisions

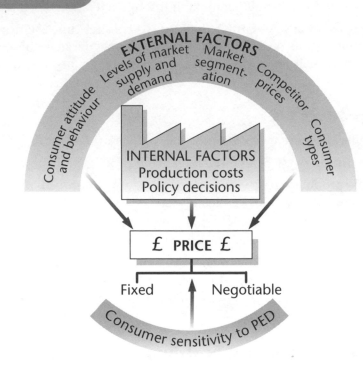

Figure 7.5 *Price influences*

Pricing methods

- Economists view price as the **interaction of supply and demand**. Many marketers regard this analysis as useful but limited, arguing that the role of other factors such as promotion is understated.

- Costs will influence price. **Cost-based pricing** uses production and other costs. An example is **cost-plus** pricing, which is based on absorption costing and takes all costs into account:

  - total fixed costs are divided by the total output to give a unit fixed cost

  - the unit variable cost is added to give the total unit cost for the product

  - a percentage (the **mark-up**) is added for profit, to give the selling price.

- **Contribution pricing** is an alternative cost-based approach. It uses marginal costing principles, calculating the contribution to total fixed costs made from each product sold. As long as the selling price exceeds the product's variable costs, it is making a contribution towards fixed costs.

- The firm uses this information to make pricing decisions, such as setting **differential prices** or selling **loss leaders**.

- Rail and airline transport is a good example: low-fare, stand-by, off-peak or customer category ('students' or 'senior citizens') pricing is used to fill seats: the marginal cost of these passengers is low, and any contribution helps cover fixed costs.

- **Market-based pricing** occurs when firms set their prices at or near the current market price.

- Where there is little product differentiation in the market and therefore a high elasticity of demand, the firm has to charge virtually the same price as competitors: where a competitor is the brand leader, the firm may have to sell at a lower price to achieve an acceptable sales level.

- The firm may try to establish a **profit-maximising** price, by taking into account the product's elasticity of demand.

Pricing strategy

- A firm may consider **psychological pricing**, setting a price to reflect the product's image and its target market expectations. Consumers expect to pay more for certain brand names (e.g. Dior, Nike, Mercedes), the high price reinforcing the quality image.

- Another psychological influence is to set a price below a key figure: e.g. £9.95 rather than £10.00.

- A **'skimming'** or **'creaming'** strategy is where a high price is set for a new, innovative product to maximise profits in the short-term.

- This is possible because the product has a **scarcity value**, the high price boosts its image and appeal, and the firm is in a temporary monopoly position. Once competitors arrive onto the market (often encouraged by the high price and profit margin), the firm will normally cut the price and focus on the mass market.

- Examples of skimming strategies are often found with technologically innovative products.

- A **penetration pricing** strategy is one of lower prices and profit margins, and is used with both new and established products.

- Penetration pricing is often used:
  - with products that are high-volume, long-life and price-sensitive
  - if the firm wishes to become market leader, has a cost advantage over its competitors, or may benefit from economies of scale.

- Penetration pricing is a useful strategy if brand loyalty can be established, but psychologically a low price can be associated with low quality in consumers' minds.

- **Predatory pricing** is a form of penetration pricing where a low price, often below the cost of production, is set in order to drive competitors out of the market. This anti-competitive strategy can be used if a conglomerate decides to **cross-subsidise** its predatory pricing in one market with profits from elsewhere.

- The benefits of penetration pricing can be quick growth, eliminating competitors from the market and discouraging new firms from entering. It is also high-risk: e.g. competitors may respond by cutting prices, resulting in a price war.

Examiner's Tip

Price represents a profit objective to the seller and a measure of value to the buyer.

Place

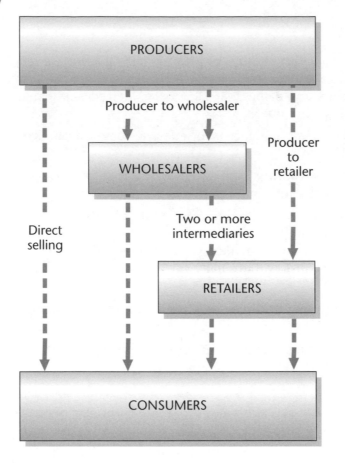

Figure 7.6 *Channels of distribution*

Good distribution delivers the correct quantity whilst maintaining quality and security. Each channel offers a level of **effectiveness** which must be offset against its **cost**. Choice of channel also depends on the degree of **outlet control** required: e.g. mass-market items are not affected by the outlet's image, whereas 'exclusive label' product manufacturers exert great control over outlets.

The channels

- Many products are sold **directly** to final consumers: e.g. 'factory shops' and many industrial goods. The seller achieves greater profit by avoiding intermediaries, and closer customer contact.
- **E-commerce** is a major development, with internet-based firms selling directly to consumers.
- The **producer-wholesaler** channel is popular with small producer firms making a limited product range.
- However, the producer loses control over the final product outlets and receives lower profit margins (compared with direct selling).
- The traditional wholesaler is not used by high-street chains (e.g. Tesco) which have their own warehouses. Other forms of **producer-retailer** link include the 'tied outlet' approach, e.g. breweries.
- The **full chain** is used where products are sold through smaller retailers. The wholesaler allows wide product distribution and cuts the producer's transport and administrative costs: but the producer lacks control over promotion, and consumer contact.

Examiner's Tip

Internet and TV-based distribution allows firms closer access to the final market, and greater access (through 24-hour trading).

Promotion

The nature of promotion

- Firms promote their products to sell them in the existing or a different market/segment, to introduce new products onto the market and to maintain or increase market share.

- A firm may also advertise to **improve corporate image**, which can positively boost its whole product range.

- The promotion mix consists of 'above-the-line' (advertising), and 'below-the-line' costs – personal selling, sales promotions and other influences such as packaging and public relations: the mix chosen depends on the relative cost and effectiveness.

- Promotion can be analysed using techniques such as AIDA: it must

  - create **awareness** of the product/brand in the market-place
  - arouse the **interest** of the consumer
  - stimulate **desire** for the product/brand in the consumer
  - provoke **action** by the consumer.

The advertising message

- Advertising is a media-delivered message **paid for by a sponsor**.

- Advertising campaigns contain information and seek to persuade.

- **Informative** advertising provides factual information about the product.

- The objective of **persuasive** advertising is to convince customers that they need the product: it includes persuading them to buy the firm's product rather than a rival one.

- Persuasive advertising is assisted by the use of branding and other forms of **product differentiation**, seeking to establish brand image and customer loyalty through persuasive statements.

- Persuasive advertising is often criticised for:

  - making outlandish claims – false claims are illegal under the Misleading Advertising Directive (EU) and the Trade Descriptions Act, and are monitored by the Advertising Standards Authority's code of practice

  - manipulating consumers – e.g. tactics involving sex or status are used to make the product more appealing.

- Ethically-aware firms will adopt advertising campaigns that avoid criticism under these headings.

The advertising medium

- Television and commercial radio stations provide **mass coverage** and are therefore suitable for mass-appeal goods.

- Drawbacks include the cost (of TV advertising), an increasing trend to channel-hop and avoid adverts, the temporary nature of the advert and the lack of selectivity of this approach.

- **Print-based media** advertising is more permanent – the advert can include a reply slip and be kept for future reference – and can provide more detail than broadcast advertisements. Advertisers can also **target** certain groups (e.g. special-interest magazines).

(Continued next page)

Promotion

- Although less expensive than TV advertising, print-based advertising lacks the impact of sound and movement.

- **Other media** include cinema advertising, the internet, posters and direct marketing such as leaflets and mailshots (i.e. direct mail, also known as 'junk mail', which indicates its low response rate).

- An **advertising campaign** puts the firm's advertising strategy into operation. Larger firms can afford to employ specialist agencies – a marketing economy of scale – to create their campaigns.

Below-the-line promotion

- Firms use **sales promotion** – short-term incentives – to encourage new purchasers to try their products, and/or to reinforce existing customers' brand loyalty. The main sales promotion techniques are:

  - **free samples** to encourage the customer to try the product, and help establish brand loyalty

  - **price reductions** and **premium offers**, e.g. the use of free gifts, discount or money-off coupons, to encourage customers to repeat the purchase

  - **loyalty cards**, used to build up company loyalty (and therefore to boost own-brand and overall sales).

  - **competitions** which act as an inducement to buy the product

  - **after-sales service** to persuade customers to buy a particular brand.

- Sales promotions can be used to gain additional market share, or for a more defensive reason (e.g. responding to a competitor).

- **Point-of-sale** (POS) advertising is used in conjunction with sales promotion. POS includes any merchandising that takes place at the point of sale: it tends to concentrate on packaging and display to provide product recognition.

- POS is particularly popular with firms selling **impulse-purchase** products such as sweets.

- Advertising is impersonal, being directed at a mass audience. A benefit from **personal selling** is that the firm can target its message to suit the recipient.

- Through individually tailoring its message, the firm has **close control** over its promotion, e.g. by employing the sales staff or agents. It also receives directly any consumer comments, and its sales staff can handle non-sales matters such as customer queries.

- The main disadvantage of personal selling is its **high cost**. Other drawbacks include typically high staff turnover and lack of continuity.

Examiner's Tip

Effective promotion relies on effective communication to tell consumers about products: the communication consists of informative and persuasive elements.

Progress check

1 How do consumer markets differ from industrial ones?

2 In what ways do marketers segment their markets?

3 How is SWOT analysis used by a firm?

4 How might a firm sample its potential market?

5 How can a firm use product differentiation in its marketing?

6 What pricing policies are available to firms?

Answers on page 92

Operations management

Organising production

Job production

- This involves the output of a **single product** to **individual specifications**: examples include the construction of a single machine tool, a ship, the Millennium Dome and the Severn Bridge.

- Firms using job production have to estimate accurately the 'three Cs': **costs**, **cashflows** and **completion date**.

- Characteristics of job production are:
  - a high-priced product made by highly skilled labour
  - using versatile equipment under central supervision.

Batch production

- A **quantity** of a product is made without using a continuous production process. Characteristics are similar to job production, although unit costs are normally lower since fixed costs are spread over the number of items in the batch.

- The production area is often organised by grouping together similar machines and processes such as welding and assembly.

- Examples include producing batches of bread and cakes, and making a number of furniture items to the same design.

Mass (or flow) production

- This involves the output of **identical**, **standardised high-demand** products using **highly specialised** inputs. Examples include cars, televisions and other 'black' and 'white' consumer durables.

- Its characteristics are:
  - a lower-priced product (compared with job production)
  - a greater proportion of semi-skilled or unskilled labour
  - high capital investment costs, offset by economies of scale
  - specialised plant and equipment
  - highly automated production lines that minimise movement
  - costs subjected to standard costing and budgetary control.

- Mass production may cause low morale through worker boredom, and production stoppages through equipment failure. This has led to the development of **lean production**.

Lean production

- Products made using mass and lean production techniques are widely found in international trade. Governments will want to ensure that their industries are competitive internationally.

- Lean production seeks to improve the use of resources in order to:
  - reduce costs and improve quality
  - increase labour productivity and capacity utilisation
  - heighten employee morale through involvement and input.

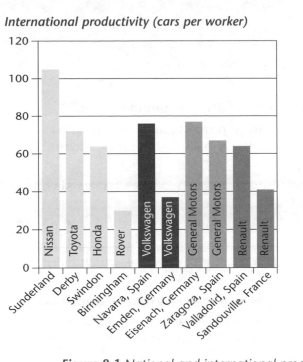

International productivity (cars per worker)

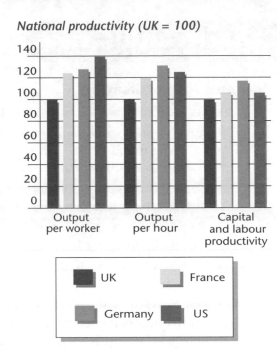

National productivity (UK = 100)

Figure 8.1 *National and international productivity, 1998*
Source (international): NIESR

Cell production

- An element in lean production, this approach divides a continuous production line into 'cells', self-contained units producing an identifiable section of the finished item.
- In this way, staff in the cell feel more involved in production.

Continuous improvement

- **Kaizen** is a Japanese philosophy that investing in employees' views and ideas is as valuable as investing in equipment.
- Kaizen groups are set up throughout the firm: e.g. a shop-floor production cell may operate as a Kaizen team. These groups meet to discuss production and other problems, and to offer solutions.
- The Kaizen philosophy stresses that an employee has two jobs: **carrying out** the job, and also looking for **ways to improve it**.
- For Kaizen to be implemented successfully, employees must:
  - be willing and motivated to make contributions
  - work in teams (such as a production cell).
- The firm's organisational culture must support its implementation.

Just-in-time (JIT)

- The JIT approach seeks to operate with a **zero buffer stock**. A firm must work closely with suppliers to obtain frequent deliveries of satisfactory-quality stocks.
- Efficient JIT should cut storage and holding costs, improve liquidity, and encourage quicker responses to market change.
- However, order processing costs rise, there is total reliance on the supplier since delivery problems will halt production.

Examiner's Tip

Successful lean production results in producing more, and making it more efficiently, by using less (fewer resources).

Capacity utilisation

High and low utilisation

- Capacity utilisation compares **actual output with maximum output**.

- A firm's productive capacity is based on its **resources**: premises, capital equipment and labour. When all are working at maximum output, the firm is operating at full capacity (100% utilisation).

- Capacity utilisation is important because a firm wants to spread its fixed costs over greater output, to reduce unit costs.

- e.g., £100 000 fixed costs spread over 20 000 output = £5 unit fixed cost; if output falls to 10 000, unit fixed cost is £10.

- Higher capacity utilisation can also lead to economies of scale, which reduce unit variable costs.

- Operating at or near full capacity makes it hard to cope with any extra work. **Additional capacity** comes through employing part-time staff (often used by particular industries, e.g. seasonal-based) and/or using extra capital resources (e.g. hire of equipment).

- Working at or near full capacity can create pressures on:
  - machinery – e.g. maintenance is difficult because the machines are always needed for production
  - employees – e.g. absenteeism caused by high workloads.

- A firm can increase utilisation by **boosting product demand**, or by **reducing excess capacity** if demand falls permanently: strategies include not replacing leavers ('natural wastage'), cutting shifts, and moving to cheaper premises or otherwise cutting fixed costs.

- Reducing capacity is often referred to as **rationalisation**.

The role of technology in productive efficiency

- The role of the production function is to **turn input into output as efficiently as possible**: a measure of the firm's **productivity**.

- **Labour** productivity is the most common measure: falling productivity makes a firm, industry or country uncompetitive, whereas rising productivity improves competitiveness.

- It is also important for **capital** to be productive. Many firms benefit from using new technologies in the production process.

  - **Computer-aided design** (CAD) packages allow product designs to be altered immediately, e.g. by using light pens.

  - **Computer-aided manufacture** (CAM) uses robotics and other forms of automation.

  - **Computer-integrated manufacture** (CIM) takes this further by integrating all aspects of production, e.g. production control with stock ordering.

- This illustrates how **capital can be substituted for labour**: whilst the firm's productivity and efficiency may improve, there is a corresponding **social cost of increased unemployment**.

Examiner's Tip

As capacity utilisation increases, unit fixed costs fall; as capacity utilisation falls, unit fixed costs rise.

Quality

Developing quality

- Quality assurance seeks to ensure **customer satisfaction** through agreeing and implementing quality standards throughout the firm.
- Quality management can be achieved through **quality circles**.
- These are employee **groups with a common interest**, which meet to discuss quality-related issues. The group consists of staff from the same production area, though it may also include specialists.
- Linked to the Kaizen philosophy, quality circles can improve product quality, and increase employee productivity and morale.

Quality control

- Quality control is an important feature of production control through its identification and scrapping of unsuitable output.
- Traditionally carried out by quality control inspectors in mass production, a recent trend has been for employees to adopt a **self-checking** approach: an example of the people-centred management philosophy, where quality is the responsibility of all.
- Quality control ensures that standards are being maintained at least. It achieves this by concentrating on:
  - **preventing** problems from arising in the first place
  - **detecting** quality problems before goods reach the customer
  - **correcting** problems and procedures
  - **improving** quality to meet improved customer expectations.
- Specific costs associated with quality control include costs of:
  - materials scrapped and labour time wasted
  - rectifying poor workmanship
  - lost customers due to defective products
  - inspection and measurement
  - training employees to monitor output quality.

Benchmarking

- Benchmarking measures a firm's production (or other activity) against **competitive industry standards**: it seeks out best practice, and managers compare this practice to that of the firm.
- By doing this, the focus is on **external competition** rather than on annual internal progress, to ensure the firm stays competitive.
- Benchmarking may operate at various levels. It:
  - provides 'market intelligence' information for the firm
  - keeps management abreast of developments
  - encourages the firm to adopt 'best practice'.
- By using benchmarking, **realistic targets** can be set; staff become more motivated through involvement and teamwork; and management is made aware of the firm's competitive disadvantage.

- Its limitations include:
  - the difficulty of choosing a suitable benchmark 'partner'
  - obtaining accurate benchmark information
  - the problem of selecting appropriate performance measures.

Quality initiatives

- This extract from Sainsbury's annual review 1999 illustrates how organisations are showing greater awareness of the importance of quality at all stages of their operations and involvement.

> **Our objectives**
>
> To provide shareholders with good financial returns by focusing on customers' needs, adding value through our expertise and innovation, and investing for future growth.
>
> To provide unrivalled value to our customers in the quality of the goods we sell, in the competitiveness of our prices and in the range of choice we offer.
>
> To achieve efficiency of operation, convenience and customer service in our stores, thereby creating as attractive and friendly a shopping environment as possible.
>
> To provide a working environment where there is a concern for the welfare of each member of staff, where all have opportunities to develop their abilities and where each is well rewarded for their contribution to the success of the business.
>
> To fulfil our responsibilities by acting with integrity, maintaining high environmental standards, and contributing to the quality of life of the community.

- There are a number of quality initiatives that an organisation can implement.
- The **International Standards Organisation** (ISO) certifies quality management by setting specifications for a quality framework, requiring firms to document procedures in a quality manual, and evaluating their quality management systems. ISO is associated with design, manufacture, installation and final inspection.
- A criticism made of ISO 9000 system is that it can be possible for a firm to set up and 'achieve' low quality standards.
- **Total Quality Management** (TQM) seeks to establish a 'quality culture' that assures the quality of work of all staff at all stages of production and sale.
- Associated with quality circles and emphasising after-sales service, TQM typifies the '**get it right first time**' philosophy.
- An example of the TQM approach is '**zero defects**', which encourages employees to develop a commitment to accurate work: there may also be financial rewards for achieving zero defects.

Examiner's Tip

Firms adopt a quality culture believing it is better to get it right in the first place than to incur the costs and delays resulting from failure.

Stock control

Purchasing and stock levels

- If stocks are too high, unnecessary **holding costs** will be incurred: these include storage and stores operation costs, interest charges on the capital tied up in the stocks, insurance costs, and any costs of deterioration, obsolescence or theft.

- Holding too little stock means the firm faces the opportunity cost of being without stock, i.e. the opportunity cost of being able to meet an order and, possibly, losing the customer to a competitor.

- Efficient stock control is based on establishing the most appropriate – the **optimum** – stock level.

- Firms will need physically to manage their stock efficiently. The oldest stock will normally be used first (stock **rotation**), and stock **wastage** must be minimised.

Figure 8.2 The purchasing balancing act

Stock control calculations

- There are four critical control levels used in keeping optimum stock.

- Reorder quantity. The **Economic Order Quantity** (EOQ) identifies the optimum order size for the stock item.

$$EOQ = \sqrt{\frac{2od}{h}}$$

where o = ordering cost of item,
  d = (annual) demand for item, and
  h = holding cost of 1 unit per annum

- If, therefore, the annual demand for an item is 5000 units, its ordering cost is £80, and the annual unit holding cost is £5:

$$EOQ = \sqrt{\frac{2(80)(5000)}{5}} = 400 \text{ units}$$

- EOQ calculations are based on a number of assumptions, i.e. that:
  - there is a constant demand for the stock item
  - there is a constant lead time (time between placing an order and receiving it)
  - stock-outs are not acceptable
  - costs of making an order are constant
  - costs of holding stock vary proportionately with the amount of stock held.
- **Reorder level.** This level triggers a reordering of stock:

  reorder level = rate of usage x maximum lead time
- **Minimum stock.** This is the **buffer** stock level:

  minimum stock = reorder level – (average usage x average lead time)
  - e.g., maximum stock is 10 000, weekly usage between 2200 and 1800, and delivery time between 4 and 8 weeks.
  - Reorder level is 17 600 (2200 x 8) and the minimum stock is 17 600 – (2000 x 6) = 5600 units.
- **Maximum stock.** This warns when stock level is at its maximum:

  maximum stock = reorder level + reorder quantity – (minimum usage x minimum lead time)
- **Stock control charts** may be constructed, to show these elements visually.

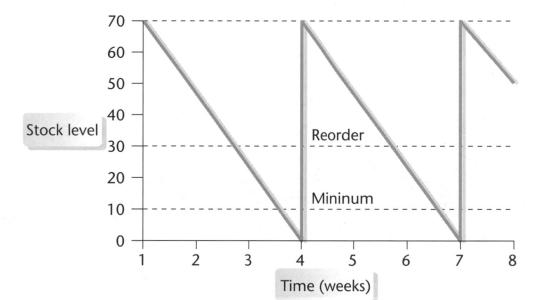

Figure 8.3 Stock control chart

Examiner's Tip

A firm holds stock to meet production requirements (materials), staff needs (consumables) and customer demand (finished goods).

Progress check

1 State the likely traditional production methods for these:

   (a) six identical houses being built on a new estate; (b) an extension to an existing house on the estate; (c) the cars owned by the householders.

2 How does a 'continuous improvement' approach operate?

3 (a) What is meant by 'just-in-time' production?

   (b) Outline briefly the benefits to be gained by firms from using this approach.

4 Outline why a firm seeks to maximise its capacity utilisation.

5 How can technological developments improve productive efficiency?

6 Why does a retailer such as Tesco need efficient stock control?

7 What costs are associated with a firm's stocks?

8 What will a firm's quality control system concentrate on?

9 What are the key differences between the ISO and the TQM approaches to quality?

Answers on page 93

Progress check answers

The business environment

1 Primary – a local farm; secondary – a car manufacturer; tertiary – a bank.

2 (a)
   (i) De-industrialisation refers to the trend away from manufacturing and construction industries towards the service sector.

   (ii) An extractive industry removes value from the land.

   (iii) Tertiary is the service sector of the UK economy, which nowadays represents about 70% of the workforce.

   (b)
   (i) The collapse in the UK of the traditional 'heavy engineering' industries such as steel (e.g. West Midlands) and shipbuilding (e.g. North-east England).

   (ii) Mining, quarrying or fishing.

   (iii) (The growth in) financial services.

3 It will increase real disposable incomes and purchasing power, increasing overall demand. If supply cannot respond, there will be price increases (inflation).

4 Demand is not responsive to price changes. The lower price is not compensated for by increased sales volume, with an overall fall in revenue.

5 Increased competition in the labour market, leading to quicker labour turnover; increased labour turnover leads to higher costs of recruitment, selection and training (e.g. induction training); a much wider range of candidates, from across the EU.

6 The goods may be necessities rather than luxuries (e.g. certain foodstuffs), or vital fuel or raw materials (e.g. coal, iron ore) not found in the home country, or unique (e.g. certain medical drugs). Without substitutes being available, their inelastic demand will lead to imports continuing at the same level.

Classification of business

1 It acts as income, i.e. the reward for enterprise; it is also a measure of success.

2 An incorporated business has a separate legal existence. An unincorporated business has no separate legal existence, and therefore legal actions must be taken (or defended) personally by the owner(s).

3 Hairdressers; plumbers; builders.

4 To gain limited liability; it is easier to obtain more capital.

5 The franchisee operates within a framework set by the franchisor – a sole trader is independent. The franchisee pays royalty to franchisor – a sole trader keeps all net profit.

6 Consumer (retail) co-operatives; producer (worker) co-operatives.

7 Corporations are owned by the state, PLCs by shareholders; corporations are controlled by a minister/board, PLCs through the Companies Acts; corporations' primary objective is normally to serve the public, PLCs normally seek to optimise profit.

8 Little consumer choice; higher prices through lack of competition.

External and other influences

1 Interest rates determine the cost of borrowing money. Exchange rates involve the relative cost of currency.

2 Cost–push: this is based on higher input (production) costs being translated into higher prices. Demand–pull: this occurs when the demand for goods exceeds their supply.

3 To meet objectives, e.g. full employment; to stay competitive internationally.

4 Financial, e.g. through grants; supply of information, e.g. on technological developments.

5 Increased costs; increased awareness of customer needs; protection against unfair practices by competitors.

6 It is in the public interest to stop consumers being exploited, e.g. by monopoly practices.

7 An ethical policy not to trade with a country because of its human rights record affects exports, and therefore sales and profits.

Structure and efficiency

1 To review existing lines of communication; for induction training.

2 Role culture focuses on a person's job role; task culture focuses on the firm's projects.

3 Span of control: the number of subordinates under a person's control. Chain of command: the flow of control (down) and information (up and down) through the organisation.

4 Managers have reduced workload, can focus on key tasks and make better decisions; subordinates gain more experience and are more highly motivated.

5 Formal: oral presentation to a group of managers; minutes of a meeting. Informal: talk about work at lunch break; informal Quality Circle meeting.

6 Larger size extends the channels of communication and chain networks: there are more layers of hierarchy through which the message must pass.

7 Horizontal: between firms in the same market and at the same stage of production. Vertical: between firms in the same market but at different stages of production.

8 Internal: based within the firm. External: available to all firms in the area.

9 Unit costs and inefficiency increase, making the firm less competitive.

Accounting and finance

1 (a) An historical statement of revenue and expenses, showing net profit;
(b) an historical statement of what a firm owns (assets) and what it owes (liabilities).

2 With leasing, the asset is never owned; in a credit sale, it is owned (after the first payment).

3 Shares receive dividends, debentures receive interest; shareholders own the firm, debenture holders are lenders only; share dividend is paid from net profit, debenture interest from gross profit.

4 Budgeting is the act of setting budgets; budgetary control compares budgeted and actual figures for decision-making purposes.

5 It indicates the likely future liquidity of the firm, enabling appropriate action to be taken if a cash shortfall is expected.

6 Total receipts are calculated: debtors pay one month after the sales so, for example, December's sales figure equals January's cash received figure.

Total payments are calculated: half of December's creditors are paid in January and half in February, and the materials figures appear as cash payments two months later; the other payments occur in the same month.

The net receipt/payment of cash is calculated for each month.

For each month, the closing cash balance is calculated from how the month's opening cash balance is affected by the net receipts or payments. Brackets indicate a negative balance.

	Jan	Feb	Mar	Apr	May	Jun
Receipts (£000):						
from debtors	150	120	600	600	400	120
from new share issue		50				
Total receipts	150	170	600	600	400	120
Payments (£000):						
to creditors/for materials	80	80	80	80	90	90
for overheads	45	45	45	45	45	45
for wages	90	90	90	90	90	90
for tax			300			
Total payments	215	215	515	215	225	225
Net monthly receipts/payments	(65)	(45)	85	385	175	(105)
Opening cash balance (£000)	60	(5)	(50)	35	420	595
Closing cash balance (£000)	(5)	(50)	35	420	595	490

7 Direct costs are directly linked to a product, e.g. materials used in manufacture; indirect are not linked, e.g. factory cleaning materials.

8 Contribution = £8.95 – £3.45 = £5.50
Break-even point = £110 000 / £5.50 = 20 000 units
(Break-even cost/revenue figure = 20 000 x £8.95 = £179 000)

People in organisations

1 To counter the loss of staff; to ensure that production and other plans can be met; to respond to a changing environment.

2 To assess: social trends (e.g. part-time working); technological developments (e.g. new skills required); economic trends (e.g. levels of pay); and political influences (e.g. changed employment regulations).

3 Through workforce planning; recruiting staff; selecting staff; training staff; and appraising staff.

4 They gain good publicity/avoid bad publicity; there will be improved employee morale; the firm's employees will lose less time through accidents.

5 Racial – the Race Relations Acts; sexual – the Sex Discrimination Acts, and the Equal Pay Act; disability – the Disability Discrimination Act.

6 In ensuring that positive hygiene factors (e.g. work conditions) and motivators (e.g. recognition) are both present for employees.

7 Management can review: pay levels, the level of employee involvement, the management styles being used, the degree of job security felt, and degree of recognition by others.

Marketing

1 In the number of customers; the channels of distribution that are used; the nature of the products; and the methods used to advertise and sell the products.

2 By product characteristics; by consumers (e.g. age, sex, income, lifestyle).

3 It analyses its internal strengths and weaknesses, and opportunities and threats in the external environment.

4 It can use a random approach; it may decide to stratify the sample; it may limit it by setting a quota.

5 Product differentiation – how consumers view products – helps firms to promote products by focusing on actual or perceived differences.

6 Cost-based pricing, which includes cost–plus and contribution forms; market-based pricing, e.g. competitive pricing; psychological pricing; profit-maximising pricing; setting a 'skimming' price; and using penetration pricing.

Operations management

1   (a) batch; (b) job; (c) mass.

2   Employee teams review problems and make suggestions for solution. Management adopts and reviews the solution in consultation with the teams.

3   (a) 'Just-in-time' is where stockholding is reduced to amounts required to just meet production demand. Tight delivery schedules are set, which may involve delivering the stock only hours or even minutes before it is needed.

    (b) A company should find that its cash flows are improved because less stock is held, and that wastage, obsolescence and the other stockholding costs are reduced. The customer gains from lower prices since the company can be more price-competitive; the company's sales and market share should therefore increase.

4   So that its costs (notably its fixed costs) are spread over maximum output; resources will also be used to their maximum efficiency.

5   Computer-aided design (CAD) improves design efficiency; computer-aided manufacture (CAM) improves manufacturing efficiency; computer-integrated manufacture (CIM) integrates all aspects of production.

6   It will seek to minimise its stockholding costs to ensure its costs remain competitive, and to guarantee that stock will be available for customers as and when required

7   Purchasing cost; opportunity cost; holding costs (wastage, obsolescence, insurance, etc.).

8   Prevention; detection; correction; improvement.

9   The ISO approach is essentially systems- and procedures-based; TQM focuses on the 'get it right first time' approach.

Index